IN CHURCH

An Introduction to Worship and Preaching

Edited by JOHN STACEY

London
The Local Preachers' Department
of the Methodist Church

Printed in Great Britain by
The Garden City Press Limited
Letchworth, Hertfordshire

SBN 7162 0173 9

Preface

IT IS sometimes said that the odds against a symposium proving a success are heavy. Presumably the fragmentary nature of a book written by eleven different people is thought to make a coherent, flowing work impossible.

With some books this is no doubt true. It is hard to imagine a successful detective novel in which one person wrote of the murder, another of the criminals in their lair, another of the detective in his police station and another of the confrontation between them. But, as students will soon discover, this is not a detective novel. It is a series of studies in worship and preaching and as such lends itself—in the judgment of the Studies Board of the Local Preachers' Department—to the symposium method.

The overall planning and the work of integration has been the responsibility of the editor. In some cases gentle pressure has been put upon authors to change their manuscripts in the interests of consistency and general policy and they have often protestingly, but always graciously, agreed. The aim of both authors and editor alike has been to produce a book which will give the student a basic expertise in conducting worship and preaching and at the same time open his eyes to the possibilities that there are in this field.

As far as the editor is aware, there are no contradictions

in the book. But there is a small number of repetitions, left in deliberately. There is something to be said in a book of this kind for two writers saying the same thing, each in his own style; it enables the author to state his case in its entirety and it provides revision material for the student for whom, sadly, this has to serve as an examination text-book.

In the bibliographies a few titles have been included more than once because they contain material relevant to more than one chapter. One or two books which are, or soon will be, out of print have also been included in the hope that they can, where necessary, be borrowed.

The Local Preachers' Department is grateful to the Rev. A. Raymond George, M.A., B.D., Principal of Richmond College, and to the Rev. Wallace H. White, a member of the Department's Studies Board, for many useful criticisms and suggestions.

Westminster, 1970   JOHN STACEY

Contents

In Church

The contributors to this book are Methodist preachers, ordained and lay. The editor is the Secretary of the Local Preachers' Department of the Methodist Church.

1. The Nature of Worship

Richard G. Jones

NOBODY reading this book should need to be reminded that few people today want to worship with us in the churches. That fact stares at us every Sunday. Moreover, the decline in church attendance appears to be going on remorselessly. We are becoming a smaller and smaller minority. This would not be quite so bad if the church-going Christians were quite clear about their beliefs and equally clear about their worship. But we live amongst a deep confusion *within* the churches, so that the task of the person leading worship becomes increasingly difficult.

Why are the people who still go to church so confused and unsure of themselves? There are at least three possible ways of answering this. Firstly, we could point to the difficulty that many modern people experience when they talk about God. They do not know how to connect up their talk about 'God' with their everyday experience of living, especially if they have been trained to find the interpretation for everything from a scientific view of the world. They seem at first to have less and less need to mention 'God' in order to explain or describe what happens in life. But this was not so with our grandfathers in the faith. If they lived in the countryside, they had a vivid sense of God's creative work all around them, and the regular pattern of the seasons and the warm companionships of the village all helped. If someone had a sudden conversion, or a mysterious dream, or a tremendous feeling of power when he prayed, all of these could be connected up with God's activity (usually quite rightly, too). It all helped to make 'God' very real. If you lived in the rough towns, it seemed as if great powers were pitted *against* you—slumps, poverty, disease, the upper classes, wars, etc.—whereas in the church life you met with a power that was *for* you. That power was obviously (and usually rightly) seen to be 'God'.

It is so different today. Few people remain in the countryside, where the farms are more and more like crop and animal factories. In the towns, most people sense man's mastery over difficulties, and have realized that psychology and social planning and advanced medicine and great technical skills have transformed modern life and helped us to build the brave new cities. At first sight, the power that now seems to be for us is our own ability to use science and technology to forge the new future for mankind. It is hard to find a place for 'God' in all this.

Secondly, there is the difficulty in finding the right pictures for God. Little children picture 'God' as a great big warm person, perhaps with a flowing beard, who sits over us all in heaven and smiles. It is not a bad picture at all. Our grandfathers in the faith did not alter it very much as they grew up, and many went all their lives with that simple, homely picture in their minds. It helped them to pray and worship and keep the faith. Little children still start off with that picture, but soon find that they have to grow out of it. Education and life in a technical society see to that. And what happens then? Bewilderment, as likely as not, because you cannot think about God without having *some* sort of picture to think with, just as you cannot think about a rose without having some sort of rose-like picture for your mind to use, a picture with which it instantly connects up whenever the word 'rose' is mentioned. So today if modern men find it impossible to have a mental picture of God, they cannot worship or pray very satisfactorily. They might find lots of words to use about God—like 'love' or 'power' or 'goodness'—but no satisfying pictures.

Thirdly, there is the current confusion about the point of our worship. Why should a group of well-dressed people go into a special building once a week in order to sing hymns and pray prayers and listen to readings and speeches? They answer in various ways. Some say that they go to meet their friends and be together; some, to escape from a humdrum life full of personal problems; some, to join in the singing and receive inspiration from the group; some, to get comfort from the sermons and possibly to be reassured by the preacher's faith, so that they can hang on to that if they have no adequate resources in themselves. But, please note, you can acquire these benefits elsewhere (the first three from a Bingo Hall, for example). If our tradition has stressed that we ought to worship because of the spiritual uplift produced ('Eh, Mary, I feel grand after that! Wasn't that singing marvellous?'), then we have no defence against our detractors who say that uplifting feelings can be obtained in other ways (e.g. drugs), so worship is out of date.

So here we are with a massive problem staring us in the face, with churches getting emptier and more and more people looking elsewhere in order to get some sort of kick out of life. What does one do? Take a stand. We view life in a special sort of way which makes more sense of it than any other, and involves some clear assumptions. We commit ourselves wholeheartedly to the belief that there is a

basic sensibleness about everything, that there is a purpose
upon which and for which the whole universe was first conceived and is still being built. Put in another way, we
believe in God. But we don't believe that 'god' is just a
happy idea in some thinker's mind, or a convenient way of
finding a solution for some haunting problems of the
human mind. We believe that the God who is the cause of
the universe and of our lives has 'got himself across' to us
in all sorts of ways (e.g. through our sense of beauty, or
through the universal sense of some things being right and
fitting and others being wrong, or through the world's
great religions), but most convincingly in the experience of
the Jews and the events that eddy around Jesus Christ—
his birth, life, teaching, death, coming to life again, continual presence in his world. To speak in a very human way
about God, it is as if in Jesus he has bared his heart to us;
that which most characterizes him is his outgoing, self-
giving, costly love. This must, then, be the real 'stuff' out
of which the universe has been created. The record of this
key event is lodged within the Bible; the result of it is
lodged in the group of people who have got the point as to
what it is all about—the Church.

In that case, how do we picture 'God'? Not as the Old
Man with a Beard who Looks Down from Heaven, but in
other more useful ways. We can picture him as the great
Father from whom everything has come and whose life
dominates all things, but in that case he is not only *above*
the world (an idea known as 'transcendence'), but also the
universe and all humanity exist *within* him. Or we can picture him as the man Jesus, thoroughly at home in our
world, totally committed to it, present in every room,
meeting us in our streets and factories, and especially
present to us in all people. This has huge consequences.
The first possible picture (Father) means that whenever we
encounter some truth about the universe we are actually

getting an insight into his 'mind'—so a scientific 'law' is a discovery about how God orders things, a new branch of knowledge is a fresh way of thinking about God's planning, and every true appreciation for life's meaning becomes shot through and through with revelation of God. Or with the second picture (Jesus) we are aware that we have been shown Real Life, Real Humanity—so that whenever we encounter something which gives worth to human living we are tangled up somehow with Jesus, with God. The whole teeming world of persons, their interests, their joys, their sorrows, their needs, their possibilities, is that in which Jesus is patently active. It is all bound up in the end with God, who is absolute lovingness.

(Notice, then, that we shall not want to connect up 'God' merely with freak experiences in life, with miracles and marvels, but with *all* experiences and most clearly with those that are orderly and regular. We shall not want to relate 'God' merely to secret insights or visions, but to *every* revelation of truth, from whatever direction it has come, and to use reason as the appropriate tool with which to handle it. We shall not want to identify 'God' merely with ecstasies and great, stirring, inspiring moments, but with *all* that has helped us to discover value in other human beings and in human existence generally.)

The great thing about being a Christian is that one has been given the opportunity to see the world as it truly is, to discern reality, to be involved with the group of people who treasure this view (i.e. the Church), and then to try to live out its implications and consequences. *That* is real living! But not many people are prepared to respond to life in this sort of way. Atheism (the belief that there is no God whatever) is becoming more and more possible to more and more people. Agnosticism (uncertainty about all religious claims) is becoming more popular. The life of the world is becoming conducted more and more on the assumption that there is no 'God' at all or that, if there is one, he makes no difference to normal living anyway (the technical term for this is the 'secular' attitude). In countless ways, at every moment, the believer is presented with a world that does not operate any more within the framework of a belief in a living God. TV programmes, plays, articles, advertisements, novels, political speeches and almost every chance conversation is conducted as if there is no supreme reality or truth about life to which the term 'God' can possibly be applied. So the believer needs the regular company of others to confirm and strengthen his faith, to celebrate the extraordinary good news that there is indeed God, that there is point and purpose to life, that there is more to life's experience than bare scientific disciplines can fathom, that there is unique value in human personality, that there is Jesus Christ at the centre of all the world's life, pointing to Real Man and Living God.

This all helps us to see the nature of Christian worship. It is not a special act put on to persuade unbelievers to share the faith; Christian worship is designed for Christian believers. It is not a device for getting believers to be a bit more inspired and warmed up about their faith, so that they may end up 'feeling better'. It is not a cosy way of running away from the real world, with all its rough-and-tumble problems and pains and rough edges. It is the Christian community's *celebration* of its faith in a Living God and a Christ who is Living Lord of his world. If someone now protests that our Church worship rarely seems like much of a celebration, we can only agree with them that much current worship is a faded substitute for the real thing, a second-hand run-down imitation. Genuine Christian worship is an exultation, a shout of delight, a paean of praise, a Great Thanksgiving for the truth and love shown to us. It involves a transforming view of the world, of oneself, of everything else. But it has strong roots, deep in history in Palestine, so that it has none of the qualities of the make-believe and the fairy story.

Whenever we are clear about this and try to plan and formulate our worship accordingly, we shall find that the other things we had hankered after (the chance to convince unbelievers, the means for emotional uplift, the chance for a pause from the harsh texture of much everyday living) are granted to us as well. They are all by-products of genuine worship. Aim at the appropriate sort of celebration, and the other will be added as well. But if we aim first at the benefits, we reduce worship to a device whereby we can screw some personal advantages out of God—which does not work. He is not mocked. He does not exist to suit the pet desires of some church-going people. Instead, we exist as a result of the awe-inspiring love whereby he is constantly creating new life and constantly giving himself to his creation.

If someone asks why we bother to celebrate this faith, we can only reply that we do it because it is true. There is no other special justification for our worship. A lover constantly tells his beloved how much he loves her, and will go on doing so as long as they live. They both know this fact, and have staked their lives upon it, but it is part of the nature of love to be constantly expressing itself, using words like 'Darling, I love you' to reiterate the basic truth upon which both are dependent. This constant repetition helps to deepen and mature that love—but its only final justification is in the fact that it is true. If, of course, the lovers were surrounded by people who regularly doubted their love, it would give even more point to the constant love-talk. Similarly, this is the final justification for Christian worship—that it is true. This *is* the world which God fathers, in which Jesus Christ is made plain, in which his dynamic love is at work to do persistent good to his children. This is the best news about the world which anyone could ever hear. It is worth celebrating, over and over again. It needs to be celebrated, because on every side there are pressures to deny it or doubt it, to shy away from its demands or to denigrate it. Christian worship is thus the regular reaffirmation of the central fact about all things and all lives and all worlds, despite all voices to the contrary.

It is an activity which requires a group of people. We never celebrate good news adequately by trying to do it on our own. A celebration is a communal, shared event, like a party or banquet or festival or great meeting or rally or jamboree or concert. You *can't* celebrate on your own. This is why worship is a community event in which the Church acts as a whole body. Of course, individuals can have worship-like experiences and moments in all sorts of situations, but they cannot *celebrate* their significance and meaning without other persons sharing. Thus Christian worship is where 'two or three are gathered', and not merely when one lone man adores his God. There is no necessity for it to be in a special building designed for it and designated as a 'church'. It can be in a front parlour or back kitchen, in the open air or, for that matter, in an aeroplane. But there are obvious advantages in having it in a setting designed for the occasion, especially if large numbers are going to be involved.

There is another way of handling this theme. Notice how the Bible records how God has constantly been working to produce a faithful *people*. Its story is not about a few holy individuals whom God has been able to use, but of their part in what the whole people of God are experiencing. As soon as anyone is converted and wants to join in with the purpose of God he becomes baptized and drawn into the people of God and their life. In that community of faith he learns what it is to be a disciple, and amongst them he celebrates the faith in worship. Christian living is not therefore a matter of seeing if I can 'get right with God' for myself and then go my own way through life, but a matter of being caught up with the new community, the Church. I shall need a pattern of personal devotion—prayer, meditation, study, Bible-reading, etc.—but I shall inevitably need to be drawn into the people of God in their experience, their worship, or I shall have missed a vital dimension of the whole life with Christ. Christian worship is a Church experience.

I The features of Christian Worship

Men have discovered, over the ages and by constant experiment, that a certain order of foods at meal-times works best and is most suitable for the human digestive system. If you invite friends in to a meal you are well advised not to start with hot coffee, proceed with cold fruit salad and ice cream, go on to hot roast pork and vegetables, washed down with insipid water, and rounded off with hot soup, fruit, then frozen fish. Similarly, Christians find that there are certain features of their worship celebration which need to be included if possible and which need to follow a simple sequence if the whole experience is to be as satisfying as possible. We can learn from that heritage of experience.

The simplest order for an act of Christian celebration is this: (1) Celebrate being in God's presence and world.

(2) Hear the news he has for us today.

(3) Make an appropriate response with our lives. Within a well-ordered service these three stages can very easily be traced—but more is said about this in chapter 4.[1]

[1] See the orders of service on pp. 68–9, where the first section is called *The Preparation.*

Our immediate purpose is to enquire more precisely into the various features involved in each of these stages.

(1) Celebrating God's presence

We begin with the celebration that we are in God's presence and world, one which exists solely because of his love for making things and people, one in which Jesus Christ is permanently alive and active to produce good for mankind despite the grip of evil and decay. We often open our worship by declaring this magnificent truth. Frequently these declarations have sounded like appeals to God to come and be with us. There is a sense in which, of course, this is absurd. God does not need to be pleaded with to come and share in our celebrations, for we were first called together by him before the worship started. It is his presence which makes the feast. Technically this element in worship is called the *invocation*,[2] and we will designate it here as feature (*a*) in the celebration of God's presence.

Then we try by songs and words and prayers to express our sense of the sheer glory of it all, the wonder of such a God. In technical Christian language, this is *adoration*[3]— feature (*b*). It is especially here that words are lamentably inadequate to express our awed awareness of the grandeur of God, and we sense their fumbling, puny capacity to express the mighty and deep responses of the human spirit. Because of this difficulty some people leading worship will completely omit acts of adoration—if you are tempted to do this, soak your mind in the Psalms, using preferably the *New English Bible* or else the translation which accompanies the Gelineau singing of the Psalms. Be discriminating, of course. Don't expect every Psalm to be equally useful, and quietly omit the ones that are bloodthirsty or self-righteous or sub-Christian (such as 59, 109, 137).

[2] See chapter 5, p. 95.
[3] See chapter 5, pp. 94–5.

Nevertheless, the glory of the psalmists was that they learnt to put into words their adoration and we, who have so much the more to adore God about as a result of his greatest deed in Jesus, can build upon their method and language and style.

Adoration moves inevitably into *confession*[4]—feature (*c*) —our sense of barren unworthiness before the glory of God, before his demonstration to us of True Man in Jesus Christ. When we contemplate him, how pathetic and shabby and self-centred do our lives appear! It is like the time when a bright shaft of sunlight comes through the window and shows up all the little specks of dust and dirt floating about in the atmosphere; the shaft makes you realize that you live and move and breathe in that dirtied setting. Likewise, to celebrate God's bright glory in Christ makes you sharply aware of your paltry, inadequate, muddled living. Because God is truth we are obliged to confess this stark truth about ourselves, we have to confess to being sinners. But there are several pitfalls to be avoided here. It is silly for us to exaggerate our sinfulness, for it is a pretence to suggest that we are the most heinous individuals who have ever existed. We are not, so let us not try to deceive anyone that we are. More dangerously, many confessions take the form of long lists of wicked *deeds* we are presumed to have done. In fact, we may not have *done* many things that were noticeably sinful. The real material about which we need to make confession is the state of our selves, rather than the deeds we have committed. Further, we are not merely dealing with the particular extent of sinfulness that applies to the small group of folk in the church. We are a sample of mankind as a whole and should be confessing the state of humanity as a whole, without any attempt to pose as if we were somehow distinct from all

[4] See chapter 5, p. 95.

other men and not caught up with them in the collective sinfulness and tangled selfishness of the human race. We are all caught up willy-nilly in the massive selfishness of the Western world, the persistent pressure for more wealth, the willingness to threaten others with nuclear war, the injustices of our unequal society. Finally, there are very special sins which apply to the Church, an *added* overtone to the others, and we are integrally part of them. We are part of the unfaith of the Church, her failure to be true to Jesus Christ and to work his works with him, her reluctance to even contemplate loving the world as he does and serving mankind as he does. We confess it.

God's first word in reply to us is always one of acceptance. 'I accept you.' It is extremely important that this should be made crystal clear in the worship, and most appropriate that this should be done immediately after we have confessed our sins. Technically, this is known as *absolution*[5]—feature (*d*). It gets us close to the very heart of the gospel. God accepts us, even though we are squalid little sinners and have repeatedly failed him. We remain his children nevertheless, and upon us he lavishes his forgiving, rebuilding love. He forgives us just as we are. This is frequently misunderstood by Christians (perhaps, in the end, because it is almost too good to be true), but to miss this point is to miss the full graciousness of the extraordinary gospel. God does *not* say 'Come, come! Put your lives right! Start saying your prayers and being more religious. Repent of your sins, clear up your relationships with your neighbours, start behaving better, and then I will take you on, I will accept you.' He *begins* his dealings with us by accepting us and *then* we can set about the huge task of building up a better life. We can see this very clearly set

[5] See chapter 5, p. 95, and the orders of service on pp. 68–9 where it is called 'Declaration of Forgiveness'.

out in the way that Jesus deals with people, as reported in the New Testament.

(2) *Hearing God's news*

Now we move on to the second main stage of worship. This is where we attend to the message that God has for us, the news by which he intends us to live. Because he is a God who is constantly at work communicating with us and dealing with us through Jesus Christ, through the Bible, the Church and all the agencies of the Holy Spirit, then in our worship we celebrate this fact and listen to what God has to say. We now rehearse the news of who God is and what he has done with us in the past, centring our attention upon his Word embedded within the Bible. Also we attend to what he is doing now in the contemporary world, what he requires of us men so that we shall be caught up faithfully in his on-going purposes and activities. It is here that preaching has its place, because in it we are really asking one or more persons to put all this into words for us. Preaching is the proclamation of what God has done for his people and what he is still doing. More will be said about it later in the book (chapters 7–11), but here we ought to note that it does not have to be limited to words only, to verbal proclamation. Truths can be imparted by other methods than merely the use of words; messages can be passed by actions, or certainties can be developed in people by the careful use of symbols or drama. So teachers today use drama or visual aids as well as instruction by words; lovers hold hands, because that utterly simple act tells each one that they belong to each other and has just as much power as words; music can be used to 'tell' people to be quiet, or be at peace, or become excited; symbols can evoke a strong emotional response from us (e.g. the way advertisers use them, so that the letter 'K' now means cornflakes, or a tiger was associated with a brand of petrol).

Within the Christian tradition certain symbols and acts have great dynamic to impart God's message to us—e.g. the use of water with baptism, or bread and wine in a symbolic meal. These highly-powered symbols also speak, but frequently with much greater effect than any string of words.

This leads us to a particularly important principle which is at work whenever we are at worship. When God's truth is 'got across' to us, by whatever means, God in himself has got across to us. Something tremendous *happens*. We normally think that when one person tells another something useful, then all that has happened is that information has passed from one to the other and no great change has taken place in the receiver. We must *not* think of worship, or of this stage of worship, in this fashion. As we saw earlier, we have no right to begin thinking of God in a detached sort of way, as if he lives a long way off and will have to shout messages to us across a great void. We live *in* God. Every way in which we have our lives opened up to his truth and exposed to his love is at the same time a way in which we become impregnated with the love and vitality of God himself—or, in technical terms, we 'receive grace'. So worship is not merely a matter of hearing truth and receiving a message, but of being encountered by God himself and gripped by him, and discovering one's life interpenetrated by his Spirit.

(3) *Making our response*

The final stage in Christian worship is our organized response to this. Frequently in the past we arranged our services so that this response could never be adequately expressed—that is, when the sermon was over, the preacher announced the last hymn and afterwards pronounced the benediction and we all went home. Worship needs to be ordered so that we can make a fitting response formally, there in church (and, of course, afterwards in the way we live). The immediate way in which we wish to respond is through a great surge of adoration and thanksgiving,[6] issuing in a new dedication of ourselves to Christ. If the proclamation has indeed been effective and made us keenly aware of the great deeds of God, then of course we will want to adore and thank him. For this reason *The Sunday Service* (and of course the traditional Communion Service) issue here into the *Sursum Corda* 'Lift up your hearts' and into the mighty prayer of thanksgiving for all God's great deeds in creating, rescuing and giving hope to the world through Jesus Christ our Lord, and in pouring out the vitality of his Holy Spirit upon mankind and through the Church.

We need to note here that we ought not to select our 'religious experiences' as the only staple items in thanksgiving—e.g. the gift of prayer, the relief of forgiveness, the news of the gospel, the fact of Christ, the existence of the Church. This introduces an artificial division into our response to life, as if it is only in the 'religious' area that God is active for our good. But he is the source of *all* that is worthwhile in life, all beauty, all that enhances human beings, all truth, all love, all that we see in Christ. Our thanksgivings need to express all this realistically. Perhaps on a typical Sunday morning we ought to be thanking God for the relief we felt when we awoke and realized that we hadn't got to work today and could take things easier; for the talk we heard on the wireless over breakfast; for the serenity in the park; for the news of a treaty bringing harmony to two rival nations; for the silvery wonder of a jet plane flying high overhead in the still sky; for the smile on the bus conductor's face; for the reassuring sense of a home to return to, a good meal and refreshment—as well

[6] See chapter 5, p. 96.

as for all the overtones given to life by our knowledge of Jesus Christ and our share in the Church and his purpose.

But of equal importance within our response is the desire to see the world in a new light—in the way that God sees it. In Michel Quoist's words, we want to 'borrow God's eyes to look at the world'. Our besetting temptation, as silly little sinners, is to see the world from our petty, selfish little viewpoint, as if our lives were the centre of the universe and all that mattered was what affected us personally. When we worship properly as Christians, we see the whole world as that which matters, that which God makes and loves, that which has been twisted and distorted by evil, that which Christ dies for and lives for, that which he is rescuing from the fatefulness of human sin and wickedness. Our response must be to give ourselves freely to the world's need and to God's service (which are two sides of the same coin). A key expression of this self-giving is in the practice of intercession,[7] of praying for others. Here we face great difficulties from the past, in which most people thought of prayer in a very elementary, childlike way, as a request to God to do something good which otherwise he would not have done, so that a new force for good is set going as a result. If that were so, prayer would be a subtle form of magic—the manipulation by human beings of superhuman forces through knowing the technique of getting them going. Christian prayer is far from magic.

Broadly speaking, there are two main understandings of prayer which are now held by Christians. One is that God uses our prayers as he uses our deeds, to heal and bless and do good in the situation for which we are praying. The intellectual difficulties involved in this view cannot be fully resolved (e.g. why does God sometimes heal and sometimes not?), but those who believe in this view do so in the

[7] See chapter 5, p. 96.

faith that what they cling to operates at a much deeper level than human minds could ever fully comprehend. The second view of prayer—to which this author confesses his own conviction—is that prayer is the Christian people's way of expressing how they too are lining themselves up with God's great and good purposes. Let us take a simple example. Suppose that we are aware of some terrible needs in Timbuktu. In our worship, we end up praying for Timbuktu and the people there and the Church there. We do not do this in the belief that perhaps, as a result, some miracle will happen in Timbuktu, but because we know that God loves the people of that place with an almighty passion, that Christ is at work there in healing, suffering and resurrection life—and we want to capture for ourselves that realization, to drive it into our awareness, to align ourselves with the new confidence which is involved in that faith. We want to look now at Timbuktu in a new way, not as some far away place that doesn't matter a scrap to us, but as yet another setting in which God is at work. The moment we grasp this point we shall be able to discover in intercessory prayer the means whereby we make a healthy response to our gospel news that God loves his world, rather than our becoming increasingly baffled by the questions like 'What difference does prayer make?' or 'Why are some prayers apparently not answered?' Prayer is not a mechanism for getting God to work, but a response from those who have discovered that he already is at work. It is an appropriate response for those who have found in the gospel the greatest celebration for men to make.

Worship must also enable us to ask God for specific aids to our own living (technically called 'petition').[8] Here we note that we believe that the mere act of asking for some mercy from God is in itself part of the act of receiving this,

[8] See chapter 5, pp. 97–8.

because God's graces towards us are not imparted in the same way as we give a parcel from one to another—e.g. A asks B for the parcel, B decides that it is right to give it, B hands it to A. In petition, the act of asking God for a quality, a factor in one's life (e.g. a calmer temper, a kinder tongue) is also the act of enjoying that grace already within one's being.

The proclamation should also result in our own abandonment to Christ (expressed in the Communion Service by our receiving the bread and wine), which again must find expression in every service. Through a prayer or a hymn or a period of silence opportunity should be given to the people to make an act of commitment and dedication[9] to God.

The celebration needs to be rounded off by a simple affirmation of faith. The 'benediction' is this. It does not *have* to be spoken by the minister or leader, since it is not a secret formula whereby grace can be conveyed to us if the right person says it. It is a glad statement of the truth which we have all been celebrating and by which we can all live—that this is a world which is impregnated with the grace of the Lord Jesus Christ, which owes its complete being to the love of God, and in which we discover the support of the Holy Spirit in our personal lives and in the existence of the Christian community, the Church. Alternatively, the benediction can be a simple sentence of dismissal, as plain as 'It is finished, Go in peace', or 'Go forth into the world in the power of the Holy Spirit to live and work to God's praise and glory' (as in *The Sunday Service*). Now we can live properly because we have got our bearings right again, we have been re-orientated, refreshed by our sharing in the celebration. We need not be afraid of the world, or of life, however grim and tough our personal situations happen to be. Christ has mastered the world.

[9] See chapter 5, p. 98.

II Worship and Mission[10]

This is God's world. His writ of love runs right through its existence. In Jesus Christ we see this most clearly and vividly. He is at work to rescue, heal, transform, raise up broken lives, establish human dignity and worth, promote reconciliation and justice, build the new family of mankind in which man trusts God utterly and loves his brother. He has summoned us into this work and this sort of living.

But there is a tragic cleavage between this view of the world and that by which many Christian congregations actually practise their existence and worship. They treat the 'world' as an essentially evil arena from which we ought to get ourselves freed as thoroughly as possible. The Church then becomes an escape centre, a little hidey-hole for battered souls. Our capacity for good will is then directed inwards, into the church circle, into building up its warmth and strength and mutual care, rather than its being directed both inwards and outwards, towards mankind as a whole. What has happened in such self-centred congregations is that a simple need of the human spirit has been exaggerated, distorted and then allowed to distort the whole ethos of the Church. That need is for regular renewal, replenishment, realignment of one's life through having a chance to stand back from one's routine through a simple process of withdrawal. We need to be with fellow Christians to do it adequately through a celebration, but the withdrawal is primarily for renewal and not for escape.

There is a critical difference between these two which we can illustrate from the simple human need to sleep. Suppose that Jack is leading a very full, purposeful, good

[10] See also chapter 7, p. 132.

life, into which he throws himself with enormous zest. At night, he is dead beat, and sleeps like a log. When he wakes up refreshed he is genuinely glad to be alive and to get back again into the exciting business of living. Jake finds life to be a bore. His work is a dreary routine which is a necessity; people tend to annoy him and get in his way. He likes to get away to bed, which gets him away from a flat, dull life; he groans when he has to get up in the morning and face another day. Now both Jack and Jake, being human, have to make regular withdrawals to bed every night, yet there is a critically different quality about their sleep—for one, bed is the means to be refreshed in order to get on with the bracing business of life, for the other it is a hideaway in which he can get lost for as long as possible.

Whenever a Christian group starts to exist merely for its own benefit, in order to be freed from responsibility for the world, it has become infected by the Jake spirit. Its 'sleep' becomes selfish and escapist, and its whole community life becomes distorted. It has lost its sense of mission, which is close to losing its soul. There is no chance of its worship being a genuine celebration—instead, it will be emphasizing its aloofness from the world, its superiority to the world, its personal possession of Christ, its own self-obsessions. In the process it will have lost sight of the scope of the gospel, ending up with a belittled Christ who only lives for the righteous. There is little health here. Unless God's people are learning from him a genuine out-reaching love for his world and for all humanity, their worship will be infected with sanctimonious humbug. It will also, in all probability, become more and more backward-looking, so that it appears as an exercise whereby twentieth-century man forgets his age and has to imagine that he is a first-century Palestinian. In this way, God's good news is transposed away from the present, into a far away event applying to an era long ago in the dim recesses of history. It will not do. The gospel is about what God is doing today for today's world.

This takes us back to where the chapter began—with the disturbing fact that few people want to worship with us today in church. If that worship is merely the tame expression by a tame group of people of their own tame concerns for themselves, then why should anyone want to join in? In the rapid and bewildering social changes through which we are living, much congregational worship has become tame, backward-looking and escapist. It does not deserve to cut much ice in such an exciting era as ours. But God is the giver of new life, the father of resurrections. Therefore he is at work with us to renew our worship and resurrect our churches and re-form our patterns of Christian living. That re-formation is actually happening, now. In it, two renewals are going on together, because they are linked intimately to each other—the renewal of worship and the rediscovery of a mission to the whole world. We cannot have one without the other, as the argument of this chapter makes plain. But if we are called to lead worship, we must therefore be, in ourselves, obedient to both the renewals and part of them.

Useful Books

Worldliness and Worship—James F. White (Oxford University Press 1967)

The Principles of Christian Worship—Raymond Abba (Oxford University Press 1957)

Worship and Mission—J. G. Davies (S.C.M. Press 1966)

The Renewal of Worship—R. C. D. Jasper (Oxford University Press 1965)

Jacob's Ladder[11]—William Nicholls (Lutterworth Press 1958)

31

Worship and Congregation[11]—W. Hahn (Lutterworth Press 1963)

Preaching and Congregation[11]—J-J von Allmen (Lutterworth Press 1962)

Worship—J-J von Allmen (Lutterworth Press 1965)

The Psalms, A New Translation (Collins, Fontana 1966)

The Sunday Service (Methodist Publishing House)

[11] Series 'Ecumenical Studies in Worship' ed. J. G. Davies and A. Raymond George.

2. The History of Worship

Robin E. Hutt

THE purpose of this chapter is to trace the development of worship from the time of the Apostles to the present day, dealing basically with the Sunday worship of the Church and the way it developed in the western world. The last part of the chapter will point to lessons that we can learn from this development and its expression in other churches.

The worship of the early Church

Christian worship involves putting into words, symbols and actions our reverence for God. It includes the corporate celebration of what God has done and how he has made himself known, as his mighty acts are brought to mind; it gives opportunity both for response to him in praise, thanks, confession and offering, and for deepening our understanding of God and his will for mankind.

As Jews, the first Christians already shared in this kind of worship in the synagogue week by week, and in the Temple. They were accustomed to meeting together to hear the Scriptures read and expounded, to pray together and to sing hymns. They would have been familiar with the worship of the Temple, which centred on the sacrifices offered to God, and which provided what Evelyn Underhill calls the 'primitive symbols and references'[1] such as 'Lamb', 'Blood' and 'Sin-offering', which New Testament writers used in describing the significance of the death and resurrection of Jesus.

The God whom they had worshipped together every Sabbath was the same God who had made himself known to them in Jesus; so after the resurrection they naturally worshipped as they had done before, but their worship had a new emphasis and content. In addition to their Temple and synagogue worship they met in private to celebrate God's saving act in the death and resurrection of Christ, by breaking bread and sharing wine in obedience to Our Lord's injunction at the Last Supper. This was a communal act, and was preceded by a communal meal called the *Agape*, or 'Love-feast'. Speaking with tongues also occurred during worship, but it had a very lowly place in the lists of spiritual gifts (ref. 1 Cor. 12:4–11, 28–31; Gal. 5:22–3) largely because it did little to instruct or edify the rest of the congregation (ref. 1 Cor. 14:1–25), and it soon declined. After Christians were banned from the synagogues, all the worship took place in private houses.

By the end of the first century the *Agape* and speaking with tongues had largely disappeared, leaving the regular form of Christian worship as the Christian adaptation of the synagogue service, plus the Lord's Supper. The first centred on the reading and exposition of Scripture (now mainly the Prophets) and the second on celebrating the death and resurrection of Jesus. The two parts, the Liturgy of the Word, and the Liturgy of the Upper Room, have formed the basis of Christian worship ever since.

From the writings of Justyn Martyr, about AD 140, we can get some idea of the pattern of early Christian worship. As the congregation assembled passages from the Prophets, Gospels and Epistles were read. A sermon expound-

---

[1] Evelyn Underhill, *Worship* (Nisbet), p. 213.

ing the reading was preached, then prayers were offered.
These prayers were usually in the form of suggested topics
(biddings), silent prayer, and a brief summarizing prayer.
A collection for the poor was taken, and bread and wine for
the Lord's Supper was brought in. At this point a long
prayer was said. It was an extempore prayer, but followed
a regular pattern, and was basically a prayer of thanksgiving. Then followed the breaking of the bread (the 'Frac-
tion'), communion and dismissal.

Here we see a balanced service, with the Liturgy of the
Word and the Liturgy of the Upper Room given their due
weight, with a place for extempore prayer within an
established framework, and with opportunity for the corporate participation of the congregation.

(*N.B.* The prayer of thanksgiving was such a charac-
teristic of the service that the elements were termed
'thanked-over' or 'thanksgiving', the Greek words giving
rise to our word 'Eucharist.' Thus the whole service came
to be referred to as the Eucharist. So when this term is used
in the rest of the chapter it will simply be as a term
generally accepted in the Church, and not used to imply
any particular doctrine or type of churchmanship.)

The worship of the medieval Church

From the end of the fourth century significant developments took place. The most startling of these was the growing reluctance of the laity to receive the elements at the
Sunday Eucharist, except at Easter. The reasons were
bound up with other developments.

By now Christianity was a permitted religion, and became the established religion of the Roman Empire.
Becoming a Christian no longer involved the risk of perse-
cution, and many more people joined the Church. Christians no longer had to keep apart from the mainstream of

secular life, and the Church was confronted with a blatantly immoral society. One reaction was an increase in celibacy and in the ascetic life, in which people consciously turned their backs on all material comforts and physical pleasures. This gave rise to a double standard, whereby Christians living normally in society could be deemed good, but those who gave up worldly things and took up a celibate and ascetic life were better. The clergy therefore came under pressure to live celibate lives. The next step was the demand for temporary celibacy for communicants before the Eucharist. This was justified by reference to 1 Samuel 21:4–5, where it is implied that the Levites had a period of celibacy before eating the Shewbread. This demand for sexual abstinence was probably a major cause of the decline in the reception of communion by the laity.

Another contributory factor emerged concerning the way people regarded the bread and wine. Warning had always been given about receiving the elements unworthily (ref. 1 Cor. 11:27), but from Cyril of Jerusalem's time (350–386) emphasis was increasingly laid on the sacrificial nature of the elements and the words and actions surrounding them. The Eucharist was seen as the presentation to God of Christ's sacrifice. Prayers of intercession, especially for the dead, were added to the prayer of thanksgiving, and the emphasis gradually shifted towards seeking forgiveness as the sacrifice was offered. The offering of these prayers was part of the function of the clergy, who were beginning to be thought of as priestly mediators between God and man. This heightening of mystery and awe surrounding the communion had its influence in making the laity reluctant to receive the elements.

In the East, where Cyril's views had their greatest effect, it became the custom to hide the elements from the congregation after they had been brought in. First a veil, and then a screen, was set up to prevent the people from seeing the actions and hearing the prayers associated with the elements. This is still so today, but there is within Eastern Orthodox worship at its best an atmosphere of mystery and holiness, and the sense of the presence of the glorified Christ.

These developments had grave effects on the worship of the Church, so that in the Medieval period we see the local community still coming together on Sundays, but taking very little active part in the worship.

In the West the Liturgy of the Word no longer functioned as a service where the Word of God was read and expounded, for lessons were in Latin (unintelligible to most) and preaching was very sporadic. Responses were taken over by choirs; and ritual actions, the use of lights, incense and rich vestments increased. The first half of the service became an elaborate pageant of music and pomp, during which the congregation watched, or engaged in private devotional practices.

The second half of the service, the Liturgy of the Upper Room, was equally in unintelligible language, and the prayers were mostly said silently, though the closing words were said aloud as the cue for the *Amen*. On most occasions the people did not communicate, so the offering of the bread and wine did not concern them, nor did the breaking of the bread (now a wafer of unleavened bread); and usually only the priest consumed it. Moreover, he had his back to the people, and this obscured his actions. Thus the only point of interest that remained was the prayer of thanksgiving, now regarded as a prayer of consecration, asking that the elements might become the body and blood of Christ. From the thirteenth century onwards the moment of consecration was emphasized by the priest raising the elements as soon as the words of consecration had been said. Bells were rung, and incense was offered—carefully so that the smoke did not obscure the view. The people adored; for them this was the climax of the service. It was known as the Elevation of the Host, from the Latin *hostia*, a victim.

So the balance of worship, beginning with the proclamation of the Word of God, bringing response in prayer and praise, leading on to the celebration of the saving death and resurrection of Christ, all involving the active participation of the people, was destroyed. Instead there was a remote, if moving, ceremony leading up to the moment when the bread turned to Christ's body, at which the congregation were merely spectators.

This was the Sunday worship the Reformers inherited.

The Reformation to the beginning of the twentieth century

The Reformation, sparked off by Luther in 1517, splintered the western Church, and the patterns of worship diversified. There was the ongoing Roman pattern; the forms developed under the influence of men like Luther in Germany, Calvin in Geneva, Zwingli in Zurich, Bucer in Strasbourg, Cranmer in England; the Puritan tradition leading into Presbyterian worship, and the development of Free Church worship. We cannot give detailed attention to every strand, but we can look at general lines of development.

The Reformation was in part a rediscovery of the Bible as the Word of God, a renewed awareness of the absolute sovereignty of God, and a new understanding of the Church as the people of God. These insights inevitably had their effect upon worship, and there was a reaction against both the outward form of the worship they inherited, and its theology. Both Luther and Calvin wanted to restore the ancient balance of Word and Sacrament. They revised the Roman liturgy: Luther by removing everything that Scripture expressly forbade; Calvin by retaining only what it expressly allowed. This meant that Calvin's worship and the churches in which it was conducted were more austere than Luther's, as is generally still the case in the Reformed and the Lutheran churches today. Both saw the reading and exposition of Scripture, and celebration of the Lord's Supper as vital elements in worship, and also advocated the use of the language of the people and their active participation. They wanted the full service of Word and Sacrament every Sunday.

Here they met with opposition from their own people, who had never received communion more than once a year. Lifelong habits of devotion are not easily broken, and despite encouragement, exhortation and argument, communion was in the main accepted only three or four times a year. Thus the primitive balance of the Liturgy of the Word and the Liturgy of the Upper Room was not restored. The emphasis of non-Roman Catholic worship was now upon preaching and instruction.

Although the English Church broke with the Roman Church under Henry VIII, the liturgy was unaltered until the reign of his son, Edward VI (1547–53). The first Book of Common Prayer was published in 1549, and was largely the work of Archbishop Thomas Cranmer. It was in English, and provided a fuller Liturgy of the Word to precede the service of Holy Communion. A weekly communion was envisaged. However, as on the Continent, so in England, communion was only celebrated quarterly. There was a sharp reaction against the 1549 book, claiming that it did not go far enough. The consequent revision of 1552 tried to remove any possibility of a sacrificial interpretation of the Eucharist; it had altars replaced by movable communion tables, and forbade vestments. Eight months after its publication, Mary came to the throne, and restored the Roman rites.

In Elizabeth's reign (1558–1603) the 1552 book was restored, but the words of administration from the 1549 book: 'The Body of Our Lord Jesus Christ which was given for thee preserve thy body and soul unto everlasting life' and the corresponding words about the Blood of Christ, were added. Further modifications in 1604 and 1662 made no fundamental differences to the liturgy, but the resulting Book of Common Prayer, although still largely the work of Cranmer, was capable of widely differing interpretations.

Publication of the various revisions of the Book of Common Prayer were accompanied by Acts of Uniformity, which enforced their exclusive use. The Act of Uniformity of 1662 resulted in 1,800 clergy giving up their livings rather than conform. These men were Puritans, a name first used in the 1560s for those who wanted to 'purify' the Church of all traces of what they called 'Roman superstition'. They were influenced by the Continental reformers, especially Calvin. Although there were disputes among Puritans about the wisdom of staying within the Church of England to reform it, or to break away (as some in fact did) it was not until 1662 that the majority of Puritans felt constrained to exclude themselves, and suffered many hardships by so doing.

It is to the Puritans that the Presbyterians and Independents (Congregationalists and Baptists) owe their origins. The Westminster Directory of Worship, issued during Cromwell's supremacy in 1644, was the formative influence in Presbyterian worship for generations. It provided a set framework with opportunity for extempore prayer. An order for Holy Communion was laid down, to be used with the ordinary Sunday service on such occasions as the Lord's Supper was celebrated. The Independents were organized as separate congregations, and although some used the Westminster Directory, in others the form and order of worship differed greatly from it. The common feature, however, was a great emphasis on preaching.

In the eighteenth century worship deteriorated considerably in the Protestant churches. This was largely due to the quality of the clergy and preachers. Some men were excellent, and the services they conducted would no doubt have been orderly and dignified, although the full diet of Word and Sacrament would only rarely have been provided. Unfortunately, however, there were a great many unworthy men. A contemporary observer wrote: 'How often in town and country do we hear our Divine Liturgy rendered wholly ridiculous by all imaginable tones, twangs, drawls . . . by twistings, contortions and consolidations of visage, squintings, blinkings, upcastings.'[2] The Free Churches were plagued with semi-literate wandering preachers, so that Wesley remarked: 'Let but a pert, self-sufficient animal that has neither sense nor grace, bawl something about Christ and His blood, or Justification by Faith, and his silly hearers cry out: "What a fine Gospel sermon." '[3] These are no doubt extreme descriptions, but they indicate the depths to which public worship had sunk in many places, with very little thought of what worship was about, and very little conception of its being an activity of the whole congregation.

The revival initiated by the Wesleys brought new life to many parts of the Church in this country, and the next chapter will deal with that part of the story. However, despite Wesley's personal views about the importance of regular communion, and about the corporate nature of the Church and the priesthood, the picture in the early nineteenth century left much to be desired. In the Free Churches there was little stress on the parts of worship other than the sermon, and salvation was conceived of in a

[2] Quoted J. H. Whitely, *Wesley's England* (Epworth), p. 302.

[3] Quoted, op. cit., p. 315.

purely individualistic way. Long extempore prayers were common, and congregational participation limited to hymn singing and saying 'Amen'. Worship was not only lacking in its content, it also appears to have been very dull, which is only to be expected if Dr Vidler's description is true that all the Christian communities, Protestant and Roman Catholic, were: '. . . dry, commonsensical, averse to "enthusiasm", acclimatized to the Age of Reason'.[4]

A new influence made itself felt in the second quarter of the century. It originated in Oxford among some clergy of the Church of England, notably John Henry Newman and John Keble. The movement which they began was known as the Oxford (or Tractarian) Movement. They sought to return, as one of their number stated, '. . . to the doctrine which the Fathers and Councils and Church universal had taught from the creeds'.[5] Its leaders were men of deep spirituality who wanted to restore some of the riches of the ancient liturgies and customs which the Church in England had discarded. The movement was seen by many as a return to Roman Catholicism, and there were bitter controversies. The present High and Low Church groupings in the Church of England derive from these developments. Nevertheless, the Oxford Movement's emphasis on order, its theology of the Church as much more than a human organization, and its attempt to enrich the worship of the Church have had a beneficial effect within both the Anglican and the Free Churches.

By the end of the nineteenth century, there were three main traditions of worship in this country. The Roman Catholic Church carried on very largely a medieval tradition. Under the influence of the Jesuits in the sixteenth century some of the extreme 'exuberances of text and

[4] A. R. Vidler, *The Church in an Age of Revolution* (Pelican), p. 40.
[5] W. P. Palmer, quoted A. R. Vidler, op. cit., p. 53.

ceremony'[6] were removed. But the Mass was still in Latin, its climax still the elevation of the Host, the participation of the laity in the liturgy slight and their reception of communion infrequent. The Church of England used the set liturgies of the Book of Common Prayer, and such is its flexibility of interpretation that all sections of the Church were able to use it without offence to their scruples. The Free Churches had orders established by custom, and not by ruling, with a wide divergence of practice and standard, and the predominant emphasis still on preaching.

Modern developments: The Liturgical Movement

While it is true that in many places worship has changed little this century, there has been a reawakening of interest in worship, which has spread throughout the denominations in the West, both Protestant and Roman Catholic. The roots of this reawakening can be found in dissatisfaction with current worship, and in a revival of the theology of the Church as the People of God, the Laos, of which clergy and laity are equally members. The direction of the ensuing developments has been towards intelligible worship which gives opportunity for the active participation of the whole congregation.

Although referred to as the Liturgical Movement, it is not an officially organized, or easily defined, group of people. It is what it is called—a movement, a stirring within the churches. Beginning in the Roman Catholic Church with the work of Guéranger in the Abbey of Solesmes, it was at first an attempt to restore the ancient liturgies. The historical link with the past, which traditional liturgies embody, is an important factor, not lightly to be discarded; hence the interest in the history of worship. However, it is

[6] A. H. Couratin, *Pelican Guide to Modern Theology*, Vol. 2, p. 233.

not a movement which seeks to turn the clock back. It is a theological movement, seeking to find the most relevant and effective ways of celebrating the Gospel, embodying contemporary man's response, and making worship into an effective means through which man can receive God's grace to meet his need to be fed and guided in his life in the world. It seeks to adapt the liturgy to the needs of today's society; and such an adaptation can only be achieved at the point where theology and liturgy, psychology and sociology, meet.[7]

In other words it is not just a question of using modern hymns and translations of the Bible, or introducing guitars and dialogue sermons. It involves a careful consideration of the nature of worship, and of God who inspires our worship; of our proper response to God, and the ways we can most fully and corporately make that response. A service which makes it difficult for the worshipper to approach God, or to receive from him, is far from the spirit of the Liturgical Movement.

The movement has expressed itself in many ways and in many places, which we can conveniently look at under three headings.

(a) Religious communities

A remarkable revival of religious community life has taken place during the last fifty years, not only in the renewal of existing orders like the Benedictines and Dominicans, but also in the growth of Protestant religious communities. As one of the influences within the Liturgical Movement has been the renewed awareness of the Church as a corporate body, it is natural that new insights into worship and its place within the life of the Church should come from these new or renewed communities. It is no coincidence that two of the early influential figures, Dom

[7] See A. H. Couratin, op. cit., p. 235.

Lambert Beauduin and Dom Ildefons Herwegen came from the Abbeys of Mont César and Maria Laach respectively. Perhaps the most famous is the Protestant community at Taizé, in Burgundy. Although fully and practically entering into the life of the surrounding neighbourhood, their life is centred in their worship, which is well-balanced and joyful, ordered yet open to insights from the experiences of other Christians. Art, music, form, movement and colour have their place. Joy, simplicity and mercy are their keywords. Their church is called the Church of the Reconciliation, and through their liturgy it is possible to be open to Christ and to one another. It is a most fruitful expression of the Liturgical Movement, and we can learn much from it.

(b) *Official Liturgical revision*

Both the Church of England and the Methodist Church are at this moment engaged in revising their liturgy. There was an unsuccessful attempt to revise the Book of Common Prayer in 1928, but now new services are being produced for experimental use, notably the Order for Holy Communion (Series 2). Methodism, too, is in the same position, with *The Sunday Service*, among others, approved for experimental use. In both of these services the balance between the Liturgy of the Word and the Liturgy of the Upper Room is preserved. Although a weekly communion is not yet the general practice in Methodism, it is becoming common for the service, when Holy Communion is planned, to be the full service of Word and Sacrament. The Presbyterian, Baptist and Congregational Churches have also produced service books, some official, others encouraged, but not officially published by the denomination. Although there is much greater freedom of choice, as to whether or not to use the set liturgies in the Free Churches, their publication and the encouragement to use them is a clear sign of the renewed awareness of the importance of sound and adequate worship. In all the churches the importance of the two pillars of Word and Sacrament is now recognized.

One of the most amazing renewals has been within the Roman Catholic Church. The Second Vatican Council approved the translation of the Mass into the language of the people, and encouraged the active participation of the laity within it. This is the fruit of thinking expressed by Pope Pius X in 1903, who wrote: 'The primary and indispensable source of the true Christian spirit is the active sharing of the faithful in the most holy mysteries and in the public and solemn prayer of the Church.'[8] It is now possible for the congregation at Mass to enter fully and with understanding into the service, using their own language, and it is by no means uncommon to find lay people leading the prayers of intercession and reading the lessons.

(c) Local experiments[9]

Experiments in worship are now common local phenomena, particularly in the Free Churches. The East Harlem Protestant Parish in New York and the Notting Hill church furnish well-known examples of how theological and social insights have renewed the worship in these churches. *Worship for Today* (see bibliography) furnishes other examples from many denominations. This publication is useful, not only for the examples it gives, but also for its comments on the form and content of the services. As indicated in an earlier paragraph, it is easy to bring in superficial changes with little thought as to their real place within a full, balanced liturgy in which the congregation can adequately participate. Nevertheless, the fact that

[8] Quoted by J. B. O'Connell, *Active Sharing in Public Worship* (Burns & Oates), p. 11.

[9] See chapter 4, Section IV.

experiments are taking place at all is an indication of the way in which the public worship of the Church is seen to have a central place within the life of the Church, and of each individual Christian.

One avowed aim of many local experiments is to make the worship intelligible and relevant to young people, and those who are not regular church-goers, as well as to the faithful. This points us to an important aspect of the Liturgical Movement. In seeking to renew our worship, the Liturgical Movement is making a vital contribution to the mission of the Church. It does so not only by trying to make the liturgy come alive for the worshippers and so engage the uncommitted who may happen to share in it, it also ensures that the mighty acts of God are commemorated and brought before the worshippers so that they can respond anew to them. A quotation from a recent publication puts it like this: 'Not only does [the liturgy] seek to put into words and actions the truth about God as understood by Christians, but it serves also to impress that truth on those who use it. Through the liturgy, the congregation, unconsciously as well as consciously, is deepened and renewed in the truths of the Christian Gospel.'[10]

We should therefore be aware of the great responsibility which lies upon all who take any part in leading public worship. There are lessons to be learned from the experience of history—and it is to some of these that we now turn.

Learning from past and present

The following five headings are not intended to be exhaustive. They point to some of the most obvious and most important lessons.

[10] H. de Candole and A. H. Couratin, *Reshaping the Liturgy* (Church Information Office), p. 2.

In Church

(a) The need for balance

This is not only the balance of Word and Sacrament, but also the balance between freedom and order, spontaneity and custom.[11] A totally prescribed liturgy can be constricting and unadaptable to local needs; on the other hand a totally free liturgy can result in very inadequate worship.

(b) The need for discipline

This follows on from the last point. The degeneration of Free Church worship in certain periods has shown that although some individuals may provide a full diet of worship, many, with free rein, provide a very impoverished worship, to the great detriment of the congregation. If the worship is totally dependent on the insights of the leader of worship and his congregation (if they have opportunity for individual expression) then that worship is likely to be inadequate. The experience of the Church through the ages and the prayers and insights of our forefathers in the faith can add immeasurably to our experience. To ignore this heritage is both irresponsible and arrogant.

(c) The need to make worship satisfying to the whole man

This will involve ensuring that the form and content of the worship is theologically sound, so that the Gospel can be fully celebrated, for this is one of man's needs. This will mean the discipline of lectionary[12] and church calendar,[13] and careful preparation. It also means that the worship must involve the worshipper at all levels. It should, as far as possible, be satisfying aesthetically, intellectually, emotionally, spiritually. These are levels at which the

[11] See chapter 3, pp. 59–60 and chapter 4, pp. 75–76.
[12] See chapter 5, p. 86 and chapter 9, p. 152.
[13] See chapter 9, pp. 156–8.

worshipper can both be met by God and respond to God. Let us not then be afraid of colour and movement and drama.

(d) *The need to make worship the activity of the whole congregation*

Christianity involves our relationship with others. Christian worship should express that relationship, otherwise the assumption is made that all that matters is *my* salvation.

(e) *The need to make worship relevant*

Christian worship should be a real meeting place of God with contemporary men and women living in a secular world.

The lesson of history is that if these needs are not met worship becomes inadequate, the worshippers fewer, dissatisfied and spiritually undernourished, and the mission of the Church impaired.

The needs point to some of the tasks for those who lead worship. The other chapters in this book will give some guidance in facing them.

Useful Books

An Outline of Christian Worship—W. D. Maxwell (Oxford University Press 1936)

Pelican Guide to Modern Theology Volume 2 (Penguin Books 1969)

Worship—Evelyn Underhill (Nisbet 1936)

Active Sharing in Public Worship (A Commentary on the chief purpose of the Second Vatican Council's Constitution on the Sacred Liturgy)—J. B. O'Connell (Burns & Oates 1964)

Common Prayer in the Church of England—D. E. W. Harrison (S.P.C.K. 1969)

In Church

The Liturgical Movement and Methodism—R. J. Billington
(Epworth 1969)
The Liturgical Movement and the Local Church—A. R.
Shands (S.C.M. Press, revised ed. 1965)
Worship for Today—ed. R. Jones (Epworth 1968)

3. The Methodist Tradition of Worship

George H. Lockett

I Wesley and Worship

JOHN Wesley once remarked to his friend Adam Clarke: 'If I were to write my own life I should begin it before I was born.' Indeed no one can understand him without going back to his parents and grandparents.

Through them, all the main streams of English spiritual life met in him. His father Samuel was an Anglican of Anglicans, all the higher because he had renounced and even denounced the Nonconformist Academy where he had been trained for the ministry. Samuel's father John and his grandfather Bartholomew were clergymen; both were ejected from their livings in 1662 by the Act of Uniformity[1] because they refused to use the 'new book' of Common Prayer. From his incomparable mother Susanna, John Wesley inherited the Puritan strain, for her father Dr Samuel Annesley (also ejected in 1662) had become a famous Presbyterian divine. She became Anglican before marriage, one reason being that she feared that nonconformity might lapse into unitarianism.

Wesley was born in an age when questionings about Tradition and Scripture, the relation between Sermon and Sacraments, and Read Prayer and Free Prayer were much

[1] See chapter 2, p. 40.

in the air. Puritans were deeply involved in these controversies, and they wanted a thoroughly reformed Church of England on Calvin's lines. So far as worship was concerned they wished to restore the simplicity, purity and spirituality of the Primitive Church. Negatively they rejected 'human' additions like vestments and symbols not specifically scriptural. Some of the greatest men of the Puritan school (like Richard Baxter) desired a synthesis of the conflicting elements, and Wesley with his superb practical sense was in many ways to achieve this.

After his conversion Wesley paid a momentous visit to the headquarters of the Moravians at Herrnhut in Bohemia; their sincerity, simplicity and joy, their communal living and care for the orphans and the old, greatly enthused him. He contrasted the 'top of the mind' religion of so many Englishmen with the 'bottom of the heart' religion of the followers of Count Zinzendorf; among them he discovered anew the meaning of practical religion. From English dissent came the stirring hymns of Watts, but the Moravians also furnished him with models for the remarkably virile Methodist hymnody which was to be.

Thus can be understood Wesley's High Sacramentalism, his revision of the Prayer Book in a Puritan direction,[2] his recovery of extempore preaching and extempore prayer (features of Puritanism), the organization of his societies

[2] The revision (of 1784) was mainly for use in America, where a strong Puritan element existed and most immigrants were unused to liturgy of any kind . . . that must colour our judgment on it. The only days apart from Sundays it specially provided for were Christmas, Good Friday and Ascension Day, for all days should be holy. Some of the Thirty-Nine Articles were expunged: Wesley altered the form of Infant Baptism and included in place of the forms for the making, ordaining and consecrating of bishops, priests and deacons, those for the ordering of superintendents, elders and deacons.

into bands and classes,[3] the lovefeasts,[4] watchnights,[5] and covenant services,[6] and perhaps most vital for the continuance of the revival, the rapturous hymn-singing.

Wesley was a High Churchman in his appreciation of Liturgy and Sacraments, but not always in his views on ministerial order or his attitude to nonconformity. He always gave great importance to the Lord's Supper; in the year 1740-1, despite great journeyings to the remotest corners of the land, he received the Sacrament ninety-eight times, and forty-five years later he did so ninety-one times. He called Methodists to the duty of constant communion (which meant every Sunday if possible); strangely enough this was one of the things which precipitated conflict with the Established Church. He had a penchant for preaching at five in the morning. These services were necessarily short. He began with a brief prayer and a hymn, preached (usually for less than half an hour) and ended with a few verses of another hymn and short prayer. He called these early services (especially when on week-days) the glory of Methodism. Obviously they were insufficient diet for proper Christian worship, so he insisted that preaching services must be at different times from those of the Parish Church where Methodists must go for the full course of worship,

[3] Small groups of believers meeting after church hours to build each other up in the faith; the bands were an inner circle ready for a stricter discipline.

[4] Fellowship meals in the Early Church in connection with the Lord's Supper (see chapter 2, p. 34). They became obsolete for centuries, but like watchnights were revived by the Moravians; alms were collected for the poor, the meal was of bread or buns with water drunk from a common cup, and the main item was spontaneous testimony.

[5] Derived from the Vigils of the Early Church: Wesley often used them on Friday nights at the time of full moon.

[6] Derived from the Puritanism of Joseph and Richard Alleine: see the introduction to the Covenant Service in the 1936 Book of Offices.

which ideally should include Communion. (Converts from nonconformity were to go to their own Sunday service.) An ideal and full Methodist Sunday would therefore begin at 5 o'clock with a preaching service, then Morning Prayer and ideally Holy Communion at the Parish Church, evensong (including sermon) in the afternoon there as well, followed by another preaching service (again with only two hymns) around 5 p.m. Rarely could this be obtained because in most parishes Communion was celebrated only three or four times a year, and when Methodists did go, they were sometimes plainly unwelcome.

Wesley desired to combine the advantages of formal printed prayers with those of free prayer. His devotion to the Prayer Book never wearied: 'I believe there is no liturgy in the world which breathes more of a solid, scriptural, rational piety than the Book of Common Prayer' (Preface to his revision). Yet he dared not confine himself to set forms. Formalism was avoided by the introduction of hymns and extempore prayers as well as exhortations, not just into the preaching services but into the Lord's Supper itself; liturgy and free prayer went together; he stood for balanced worship. Similarly Sacramental and Evangelical were complementary. Two great demands were laid on Early Methodists: 'Go to the Lord's Table once a week' (the first rule of the Bands); 'You have nothing to do but to save souls'.

Simplicity, joy and triumph were vital notes in Methodist services. No one can understand Wesley's ideas of worship until he has read the preface to the 1779 hymn book which is fortunately printed in the present one. The hymns were an essential part of corporate worship, an ideal tool for evangelism and doctrinal teaching. The Congregationalist B. L. Manning wrote the perfect eulogy on them: 'This little book (of 1779) ranks in Christian literature with the Psalms, the Book of Common Prayer, the Canon of the Mass . . . there is the solid structure of historic dogma, there is the passionate thrill of present experience, but there is too the glory of a mystic sunlight coming from another world.'[7]

II Development since Wesley

Wesley's death in 1791 inevitably meant the end of the system whereby the staple diet of Methodist worship was supplied by the Parish Church, supplemented by evangelistic services, with hymns, extempore prayer and forceful preaching and testimonies. By this time probably the majority of Methodists (never having had much personal commitment to it) were chafing at this dependence on the Established Church. The widening gap separating Methodists and Anglicans was marked even in Wesley's day by the ninety or so preaching places where provision for all except sacramental services was made. By 1795 the Sacrament could be administered in their own chapels by their own preachers if a majority of leaders and trustees agreed. Opinion was to a degree still divided, for there remained 'Church Methodists', fundamentally Anglican in outlook who sought to prevent complete separation, and who were very suspicious of the radical policies (political as well as ecclesiastical) involved in Dissent. The ruling party among the Wesleyans, dominated for half a century by Jabez Bunting, was eager to retain the Prayer Book, and regarded Wesley's mode of worship, uniting the advantages of a liturgy with extempore prayer, as ideal.

In the 1850s many city churches continued to use Morning Prayer in a form almost identical with that of the Church of England, but in the country services were the same as nonconfirmist ones, save perhaps for the calendar of lessons. Evening services began in Wesley's time, and

[7] *The Hymns of Wesley and Watts* (Epworth 1942), pp. 14, 29.

became more and more popular, and were always non-liturgical. The Wesleyans invariably followed the Book of Common Prayer, or Wesley's revision, for the Lord's Supper. No service book was introduced into Primitive Methodism until 1861, and other Methodist bodies were all to the left of the Wesleyans in this matter.

How can we account for the weakening of the prayer-book heritage? As Methodism expanded a simpler service came to predominate; the new converts, often already prejudiced against the Established Church, and having no ties with it, began to feel that the archaic and stately language of 1662 was too remote from life. They said that they found it difficult to enter into prayers read from a book. The popular demand was for a freer type of service, and though ministers often tried to resist it, on the whole they failed. The emergence of new Methodist bodies, more democratic than the Wesleyans, hastened the process. The Oxford Movement[8] really clinched things. Dr. Gordon Rupp writes of it, 'It was soon to turn its attack with special vehemence upon the Methodists, doing more than any other single factor to provoke the alliance of Methodism with the Free Churches, and driving later Methodism in its own self-defence and in its apprehensions of a renascent Popery, from its old middle position.'[9] Sociological factors like controversy over Church and State, and resentment against such things as tithes, contributed to the hostility towards anything 'Anglican', so even Wesleyans began to move gradually but inexorably towards Dissent and its ways of worship. It must be emphasized that the Prayer Book tradition has never been lost. The first order of Communion in the 1936 Book of Offices is (with only slight alteration) that of the 1662 Prayer Book; still a few churches use the Order of Morning

[8] See chapter 2, p. 42.

[9] *Thomas Jackson, Methodist Patriarch* (Epworth 1954), p. 22.

Prayer; there always has been a minority among us who prefer 'liturgy'; overseas in many areas of ex-Wesleyan mission Prayer Book services were and are the norm for morning worship.

Quarterly lovefeasts survived to some degree within all branches of Methodism for perhaps a century. Watch-night services have disappeared entirely except as an annual occasion, marking the transition from the old year to the new. The Covenant Service has endured, and perhaps may find a new lease of life through its increasing acceptance outside Methodism.

The first preaching-house was the New Room at Bristol and was licensed in 1748. In the next forty years many chapels were licensed, but the next century was the great age of building; indeed, so prolific was the growth and so great the pace that such an establishment figure as Bunting questioned the wisdom of such 'duplication of buildings'. At the 1841 Conference when he learned that eight hundred chapels had been built in the previous five years, he cautioned, 'fewer chapels and more horses would save more souls. I think we are forsaking our calling. We should preach in barns, the cottages of the poor, and out of doors'.[10]

As the nineteenth century went on the Free Churches and all the Methodist bodies became more and more respectable, with the Wesleyans some way ahead of the rest. The urge grew to emulate Anglicanism. In cities Gothic architecture became the fashion; services became more dignified; the zealous Hallelujah and the fervent Amen were felt to be out of place; chants and read prayers were found to be in place. Perhaps with the increase in dignity, spiritual ardour decreased. This should however be contrasted with the popularity of services in the

[10] Benjamin Gregory, *Sidelights on the Conflicts of Methodism. 1827–1852*, p. 315. (Cassell 1898)

mammoth Central Halls in the first thirty years of the next century.

Until after the Second World War little change came over worship. Methodist Union made little difference except that those of non-Wesleyan background had some chance to appreciate Cranmer's Order for the Lord's Supper, and all parties were more often than not subjected to the Alternative Order in the 1936 Book of Offices. This was supposed to help those unused to any kind of service book; its one act of genius is the introduction of two verses of Wesley's Easter Hymn in the post-communion.

In the thirties voices were raised against the slipshod nature of much worship; sometimes everything else was regarded as 'preliminary' to the sermon; the 'long' prayer seemed not infrequently to be addressed more to the congregation than to God; the notes of joy, simplicity and triumph were sometimes absent; not always were the essential elements of adoration, confession, declaration of forgiveness, thanksgiving, intercession petition and dedication to be found in the praise. Although there was enough to criticize, there were signs heralding a new day. *Divine Worship* published in 1936 was a move in the right direction, but it is a somewhat mixed-up and verbose book. It was not, however, introduced into many churches, but probably helped preachers in their preparation. The Music Society with leaders like Luke Wiseman, G. F. Brockless and F. B. Westbrook did much to raise musical standards. The emphasis by men like Hugh Price Hughes and Scott Lidgett on Methodism's place within the Church Universal, of whose infinite heritage we all partake, was bearing fruit. The Methodist Sacramental Fellowship was inaugurated in 1935, with A. E. Whitham as its first President. It seeks to ensure basic doctrinal teaching in church life, to work for reunion, and to recover the centrality of the Lord's Supper. Its members accept a devotional discipline and its influence over the years has been quite disproportionate to its numerical strength.

III   Modern Trends

Since the war scholars have discovered afresh the importance of the Reformation and we are recovering the insights which Wesley learned from the New Testament and the Early Church, just as the Reformers did. In this Ecumenical Age and inspired by the Liturgical Movement[11] we find a remarkable convergence of Roman, Anglican and Reformed traditions; in going back to the beginnings we find each other at the same place, and so are becoming one. In the service books being issued by all the churches there is unanimity on most of the matters discussed below.

New ideas take time to win their way into the Church's life. A widely distributed pamphlet issued in 1946, *The Message and Mission of Methodism*, has a section on worship. It is conservative and conventional, and though it declares Holy Communion to be 'a central act' of worship it has no word about its possible more frequent observance. A report of a Conference Committee on Christian Worship published in 1960 is something of a compromise document, but it does anticipate some of the principles which lie behind *The Sunday Service*.

Let us look at some of the subjects which are alive for us in the 1970s.

There is the question of the balance between spontaneity and order. Liturgical forms have three advantages over free prayer. The congregation is liberated from dependence on the preacher, his moods and limitations; it can be involved more fully in the service; it can share in the universal heritage of prayer of all the ages. At the same time the

[11] See chapter 2, pp. 43–7.

value of free prayer must not be discounted. Its immediacy and fervour complement the universal qualities of a liturgy; on occasion it can still be most impressive. The astonishing growth of Pentecostalism, theologically naïve as it may be, is a judgment on mainstream Christianity, for the intimacy, joy and warmth of its worship is so reminiscent of the early days of Methodism, and of so many other churches. It is vital that the balance between order and freedom shall be maintained. They are not opposites, but complementary to one another.

We realize now, that worship must be relevant to daily life. Widely differing expressions of this principle are to be found in the house-church, the team and group ministry and the work of such communities as those of Taizé and Iona. Still, all too often worship seems to indicate that God has been more or less inactive since II Peter was finished about AD 135. There are however saints in the twentieth century whom we should be commemorating in worship; and if there were readings from and about them[12] as well as lections from the Bible, the exercise would come to life. Think of a passage like the last paragraph of Schweitzer's *Quest of the Historical Jesus* or the peroration in Martin Luther King's sermon before his martyrdom. To ignore the work of the Holy Spirit in our own age would be idolatry indeed.

In music new forces are at work. Beaumont's Folk Mass appeared in 1956; he and Michael Williams are among those who have put new tunes to old hymns. Sydney Carter, Donald Swann and Geoffrey Ainger are showing how contemporary folk-song can be baptized. A supplement to our Hymn Book, *Hymns and Songs*, which contains both traditional and modern tunes and words came in 1969. To use Joseph Gelineau's edition of the Psalms in which he tries to recapture the basic rhythm of the Hebrew

[12] See chapter 5, p. 87.

text, and sets it to the simplest melodies, is perhaps the best way by which the Psalms can be restored to modern congregational use.

The insight illustrated by the removal of the communion table away from wall or pulpit, so that the minister can stand behind it, the bringing of it out into the centre so that worshippers can surround it, proclaims that worship is essentially corporate action and not a show put on at one end of the building for the edification of people at the other. This links up naturally with the modern actor's concept of 'theatre in the round' involving the whole audience in the action. The recovery of the Christian Year[13] (itself a drama) must be seen in the light of experiments made to dramatize the Gospel by such presentations as *A Man Dies* or the services devised by Brian Frost with a Christian Aid theme in mind. Some publishers produce admirable collections of such services in the contemporary mood. Worship is not a matter of hearing and speaking only.

We have not progressed far in our appreciation of the value of silent prayer. Bidding prayers must involve brief periods of silence, and the latter are often mentioned in *Divine Worship*. They have a definite part too in *The Sunday Service*, but people are not trained in their use. Perhaps the experience of silence in Retreats will be a way forward.

There is a greater sense of the central importance of the Sacraments; no longer is the Lord's Supper a mere addendum, nor is it primarily now a memorial of a crucified martyr, but the means of incorporation into Christ's mystical Body and the chief means of grace. The Sacrament of Baptism is, one hopes, no longer celebrated in private or in Sunday School, but always as part of the main act of worship on a Sunday in the presence of the whole congregation.

[13] See chapter 9, pp. 156–8.

We are realizing afresh the importance of Family Worship; the presence of the Junior Church for the first quarter of morning worship must compel us to examine our methods of winning children and youth to the Faith. The Youth Department's scheme for integrated teaching and worship for every age-group presents exciting possibilities.

What to do with the Second Service is a question still to be answered. People are voting (by absence) against two services of the same kind on Sunday. Shall we gradually tend to the American way of morning worship preceded by a teaching session for all groups and nothing afterwards, or shall we make the less popular service time (usually evening) one for experiment?

As the Church moves into unity the fusing of different traditions will enable progress to be made in experiment. We can surmize that no prescribed, invariable form will ever again prevail. We cannot compel people to worship in any particular way. Diversity is the way ahead. We shall go on learning, and the more the congregation is itself involved in making the patterns of its own services the more truly corporate our worship will be.

IV The Sunday Service

In the last decade the Churches have been revising their service books and it is remarkable to see that all, from Roman Catholic to Baptist, have produced orders for the Lord's Supper on similar lines. The ideal of a conjoint celebration of Word and Sacrament, as in the Primitive Church, which was so dear to Wesley's heart, is recognized.

A quick look at *The Sunday Service* authorized for experimental use by the 1968 Conference will show how the principles of liturgical reform have been acted upon.[14]

[14] For a commentary see John Stacey, 'The Preaching Service', *Preacher's Handbook, No. 11*, ch. 9 (Epworth 1969).

Congregational participation is ensured; the offer of the Gospel and the believer's response are made very clear. In *The Preaching Service* (the first part of *The Sunday Service*) the sermon which expounds the Word remains as the great moment of God speaking, coming, offering himself to the people; their response is spoken in what follows in the service and then is acted out at the kitchen sink and the office desk, in the factory and on the farm during the coming week. So the sermon comes immediately after the lessons with the intercessions in their proper place: 'after minds have been kindled, vision broadened, and sympathies shared by the preaching of the Gospel'.[17] *The Preaching Service* is a well-structured order in its own right without the Lord's Supper. The proximity of lessons and sermon should encourage the use of the lectionary and exegetical preaching. Attention must be drawn to *Collects, Lessons and Psalms* with the new lectionary and other improvements, produced by our Publishing House. The Order for the Lord's Supper is enriched by the influence of the combined Liturgical and Ecumenical Movements. It brings out the meaning of the Sacrament as at once Thanksgiving, Memorial, Sacrifice, Communion and anticipation of the eternal Messianic banquet; there is the great symbolic act of the Breaking of Bread. It is to be noted that there are more 'may' and 'or' than 'shall' rubrics; there is opportunity for extempore prayers. Thus great freedom in the conduct of the service is attained and more people can share in the leading of worship.

The local preacher will, it is hoped, want to use *The Preaching Service* himself. Perhaps the layman's privilege of sharing in the distribution of the elements which Anglicans enjoy, and which was common in non-Wesleyan sections of the Church before Union, will be increasingly realized.

[15] John Marsh, *A Book of Public Worship* (O.U.P. 1948)

V The place of the Local Preacher

There have been Methodist local preachers since Wesley appointed John Cennick to preach to the Kingswood colliers in 1739 and to understand their importance in Methodism we must briefly trace their history. Wherever Wesley went he left societies of converts behind him under the care of class-leaders. Such men as were qualified became 'exhorters' 'to stand in the gap and keep the trembling sheep together'. They operated locally, leading prayer meetings and addressing classes. Later, as circuit life developed, suitable men preached in the chapels as the 'assistant' or superintendent decided. Often they were men of great ability and some attended Wesley's annual conferences. From their ranks usually Wesley drew the travelling preachers, whom he appointed to the circuits annually.

Methodism from the earliest beginnings depended on the local preacher for most services of worship, but organization was slow to develop. In the 1780s the first printed Circuit plans began to appear. Quarterly local preachers' meetings were not formally recognized until 1796, but by 1825 some features of our system were in being and preachers were assisted in their studies by books at special rates. Amongst Bible Christians and Primitives the local preacher was often only different from the travelling preacher in that he was 'local' and received no allowance. But in Wesleyanism there was a difference of status and function, 'occasional preaching did not impart the ministerial character to a secular man nor qualify him to administer the holy sacraments.'[17]

All Methodist bodies came to take preacher training

[17] John Beecham, *An Essay on the Constitution of Wesleyan Methodism*, p. 114, 1851.

seriously, but it was 1936 before compulsory written examinations were held.

Despite his own mother's glorious example Wesley never encouraged women to preach, and the Wesleyans (always last in such things) allowed women to come on the plan on the same conditions as men only in 1918. Nearly a century before, the Bible Christians and the Primitives actually had women itinerants. Since Methodist Union the proportion of women preachers to men has continually risen.

There has been much debate about the future of the local preacher. We must welcome the possibility that more pastoral responsibility may well be given to the qualified preacher in future, and we should be false to all our past if we did not insist that he will always have a vital part to play in the Church's life. We can have no time for the idea that he is a mere stop-gap and second-best to the full-time minister. Methodism has not, for nearly two centuries, depended on him for the conduct of seven out of ten services just because there were insufficient ministers to go round. We believe that there are insights into the meaning of the Gospel which only come to preachers who are deeply involved in the running of garages, mills, homes, trade unions, schools and hospitals. For the inefficient, careless, bookless preacher there is no future, but the Church cannot do without the one who has been truly called, and is totally committed.

Useful Books

Sacrament of the Lord's Supper in Early Methodism—John C. Bowmer (A. & C. Black 1951)
The Lord's Supper in Methodism 1791–1960—John C. Bowmer (Epworth 1961)

Worship and Theology in England Vols. iii, iv, v—Horton Davies (Oxford University Press 1961, 1962, 1965)

A History of the Methodist Church in Great Britain Vol. i—ed. R. E. Davies and E. G. Rupp (Epworth 1965)

Wesleyan and Tractarian Worship—Trevor Dearing (Epworth/S.P.C.K. 1966)

Vital Elements of Public Worship—J. E. Rattenbury (Epworth 1936)

News from Notting Hill—Mason, Ainger and Denny (Epworth 1967)

4. Ordering Services

Frank Godfrey

'HERE is an hour' says the congregation to the preacher, 'plan our use of it so that the needs of worship may be met'. What are the 'needs of worship'? A glance at the opening chapter reminds us that worship can be described as *celebration*. Christians come together to celebrate him who is the ultimate reality, God who is made known in Jesus and revealed through Bible and Church, who is the living Lord of our present life. We cannot *order* a man to celebrate, for celebration is the willing response of the spirit of men. What we can do is create the conditions in which it will become possible for men to celebrate. The principal condition is that there must be a declaration and acknowledgment of the intiative and glory of God who himself calls out our response.

I Celebration is Man's response to God's activity

Christian worship therefore includes recollection and response. As we celebrate we recall the presence of God, the formative impact of his character (Name) on human history, and his initiative in Creation and Providence. We rehearse our salvation history with its prophetic inspiration and historic events, above all in the gift of the life, teaching, redemptive suffering and triumphant resurrection of Jesus; in the giving of the Holy Spirit and the birth of the Church.

These events interpret our present existence, showing us who we are, and to whom we belong. It is our reasonable response to remember them in praise and thanksgiving, to believe in the creator of them as we say the creeds, to let our lives be amended and redirected by them in repentance and obedience, to dedicate ourselves to God in offering.

We find this pattern of God's initiative and man's response expressed in many parts of a service; each hymn or prayer may contain both aspects. But traditionally it has been found helpful to make this pattern boldly clear in the very ordering of the service.[1] Some items (lessons and sermon) are primarily declaring what God has done. Others (creed, offering, hymns and prayers of thanksgiving, adoration, intercession, petition, and dedication) are expressions of our response of obedience and faith.

The Preaching Service, the first part of *The Sunday Service*, authorized for use by the Conference shows these two parts—with the Preparation—clearly:

The Preparation	Introit or Hymn First Prayer—of invocation or adoration Commandments Confession and declaration of forgiveness Hymn or Gloria in Excelsis
The Ministry of the Word	Collect of the day Readings from Scripture Sermon Hymn

[1] See chapter 1, p. 19.

The Response
of the
Congregation
{
Announcements
Offering
Prayer of Thanksgiving for Creation
    and Redemption
Dedication
Intercessions[2]
Lord's Prayer
Hymn
Benediction
}

An alternative order expressing the principles enunciated in this book would be:

The Preparation
{
Call to worship (Invocation)
Hymn of Adoration
Confession
Declaration of forgiveness
Psalm
Anthem
}

The Ministry
of the Word
{
First Lesson
Hymn
Second Lesson
Sermon
Silence
}

The Response
of the
Congregation
{
Creed
Hymn
Notices, Offering
Prayers of Thanksgiving and Adoration
Prayers of Intercession, Petition and
    Dedication
Lord's Prayer
Hymn
Benediction
}

[2] Or the order of these three can be Intercessions, Thanksgiving, Dedication. See *The Sunday Service*, p. 7.

The weakness of our traditional order of Methodist worship (which we do not need to outline here) is that in placing the sermon at the close of the service there is no adequate opportunity for congregational response to the Word preached in the sermon.

II Celebration means participation[3]

Worship is the corporate act of the whole body, not merely the activity of a number of isolated individuals. The preacher's task is to enable the Family of God to share in the celebration. A great deal depends on the preacher's sensitivity to the Spirit of God and also to the spirit of his congregation. It is his priestly task to sense the unspoken cries of his congregation and to find the words which express and meet them in prayer and scripture, and which enable his people to participate in spirit.

(a) Sharing in the Action

One aim of the Liturgical Movement has been to bring the congregation into *active* participation in worship, rather than leave them as listeners and spectators. In Methodism participation has been in the hymns, Lord's Prayer, offering, and occasional *Amens*. In the hymns our people were able to share in all aspects of worship with enthusiasm and meaning; but increasingly the words, symbols and indeed the theology of some of our hymns no longer provide such an adequate means of celebration. The new Supplementary hymns encourage us to see what may yet come to help us, but meanwhile we should make use of other ways to introduce active congregational sharing. The preacher should consider whether it is possible—

—to invite members of the congregation to read the lessons—with adequate forewarning;

[3] See chapter 7, pp. 129–131.

—to use the psalms and canticles at the back of the hymnbook for public response;
—so to construct the prayers that they both provoke the mind to creative thought and call for a spoken response;[4]
—to create a sermon form which will allow for the experiences and questions of the congregation to be expressed.

In some churches it would be a good beginning to encourage the congregation just to say 'Amen' with freedom and conviction when sharing a prayer, or to stand in the moment when the offering—which includes the offering of each person—is dedicated.

(b) *Participation in Dialogue*[5]

The popularity of the prayers of Michel Quoist suggests that there are worship processes in which men want to share. These prayers sensitively articulate the mental and spiritual struggles which are part of the life of modern man: they blend doubt and belief, confession and praise, thanksgiving and grief into a harmony of celebration. There is no reason why such resources should not be used in worship, nor why a preacher should not contribute his own written and responsive meditations. To begin with, why not try adapting Quoist's meditation on 'Suffering'[6] as a dialogue between leader and congregation.

L. Lord, suffering disturbs me, oppresses me.
   I don't understand why you allow it.
      C. Why, Lord?
L. Why this innocent child who has been moaning for a week, horribly burned?

[4] See also chapter 5.
[5] See chapter 7, pp. 128–9.
[6] 'The Hospital', *Prayers of Life*, p. 65.

> **C.** This man who has been dying for three days
> and nights calling for his mother?

L. This woman with cancer. . . .

The dialogue leads, psalm-like, to a conclusion of faith and hope.

Dialogues need not begin only from life situations; they can arise from passages of scripture or in relation to festive occasions. E.g. Interpretation of Scripture:

L. Who is your neighbour?
> **C.** The family that lives next door.
>> **L.** The girl who serves you at the counter.
>> **C.** The man who empties my dustbin.
> **L.** The coalman, the milkman.
>> **C.** Each is my neighbour. . . .

After acknowledging the breadth of this concept of 'neighbour' we hear the command,

L. Jesus said 'Love your neighbour'.
> **C.** But this is sometimes hard . . . our neigh-
> bours can be rude or demanding, critical or
> interfering.

L. Jesus said, 'Love your neighbours as you love
yourselves . . .'
> **C.** We love ourselves though we do not always
> like ourselves. . . .

—and we are led to the great command to love our neighbours 'as Jesus loved you' and our need of his gracious loving of us.

Note how such a dialogue can provide a means for the proclamation of the gospel, for the confession of our true state, for the expression of praise, thanksgiving, intercession, petition, dedication, and for a teaching ministry. It can be an act of celebration.

There is a great wealth of worship material yet to be created in 'frozen' (i.e. written rather than spontaneous) dialogues. Perhaps the countless hymns will one day be paralleled by countless dialogues? Perhaps dialogue will signify to Methodists far more than the repetition of

L. The Lord be with you,
C. And with Thy spirit.

RULES FOR THE USE OF DIALOGUES

1. They should not be too long, ideally between 30–50 lines.

2. The theme and pattern should be simple and clear. It should not be a struggle for the congregation to understand the meaning.

3. Congregational responses should not be lengthy, and should be carefully phrased so as to be expressed naturally by all the members of the congregation.

4. Dialogues should not be motivated by our desire to indoctrinate the congregation with our point of view, but by our responsibility to create a means whereby the congregation can commit itself in active worship.

5. Dialogues are not a way of publicising literary gifts. A 'purple passage' dear to our pride may well chill the spirit of the congregation.

The writing of dialogues, like the writing of prayers and sermons could prove a salutory discipline for a preacher.

(c) *Participation through Testimonies*

The tradition of giving testimony to the saving power of Christ in a man's life has been honoured in our church, and is still followed in some places, notably on Young Peoples' Day. It has tended to fall into dishonour for several reasons. Many a man talking about God and *himself* has fallen into some subtle snare of pride. Repeated testimonies have become stale to the congregation and accrued the trappings of a 'performance'. Testimonies have been misused in manipulating a congregation rather than in celebrating God. They have focused on emotional rewards rather than dedication of the will.

Yet an authentic testimony is of the nature of a contemporary scripture; it is the word of God written large in the experience of men. Through such a testimony others may clarify what is happening in their own lives in a way they have not recognized before. To be reminded in this way of the present activity of God can prove provocative for the uncommitted and encouraging to the depressed.

By 'giving a testimony' we do not just mean a young person speaking on 'what Christ means to me'. We include the reflections of an elderly Christian, the travails of the mother bringing up her family or the father trying to work out his faith in the factory. Nor is a testimony necessarily a success story. Three men once speaking on the moral problems they faced as Christians in the cut and thrust of industrial and commercial life had each chosen a different answer, none obviously successful, but the release and encouragement which came to that meeting were quite noticeable. Some churches have a 'spot' in the liturgy for someone working in the community to speak briefly on his work and problems. This creates the possibility of more intelligent prayer and more understanding of what relevant Christian mission means.

(d) *Participation in discovering the Word*

Sharing in testimony is a short step from sharing in the *discovery* of the word to be shared. In our complex modern society the congregation can not only listen to and help to declare the Word, it can share in discovering that Word. Who but a group of housewives can help the preacher to understand what 'Bread of Life' or 'Daily Bread' can mean for housewives? What does the celebration of God mean to a group of teachers feeling the early effects of a comprehensive system, rapidly changing educational techniques and philosophy, and some early effects of non-directive approaches and the permissive society? A sharing of the experience of such groups as these may be necessary for the relevant word to be discovered.

The first Christian sermon (Acts 2:14 ff.) was not written by a man on his own, but was a sharing of the product of the Apostolic community; it was created, clarified and confirmed within Peter's experience of the Apostolic fellowship, from the crucifixion and resurrection through to Pentecost. Here is a royal precedent for the sermon to be created by a group.

In this way the preacher can ensure that his words can ring true to the experience of those who are personally involved in the situation. He can arrange for questions to be created and presented by his congregation, or reduce the length of his sermon to allow the congregation to respond in free discussion of its theme.

III Celebration requires formality and freedom

The Christian family needs formalities in its celebrations. A framework of familiar order, familiar acts and familiar words is a means of grace whereby people are helped to overcome the anxieties and confusions that can bedevil religious services. Such formality should be seen as a condition for the expression of freedom. Within the accepted order a congregation becomes free to worship.

The Methodist preacher who appreciates the pattern, can become a free man. He is not bound to use a prayer book, nor is he bound not to use it. He can provide for his congregation both the prayers and testimonies of saints of other days, and the prayers that spring from present experience.

In every age men have found that the Collect for purity at the start of the Communion service ('Almighty God, to whom all hearts be open . . .') has expressed how they stand before God; that the psalms have carried their cries of grief, perplexity and faith, and the Magnificat and Benedictus their cries of hope. All these have been born in history and thereby call the preacher to be free to speak from his *own* history as well.

IV   Experiments in services

As Methodists we have claimed to have two traditions not one: that we are debtors both to the Anglican communion from which we sprang and to the Free Churches amongst whom we found a natural home, but we have rarely taken advantage of this freedom. Attempts to experiment with worship can often be thwarted by barren controversy. Ought we to exchange the old and proved ways for the new and the untried? Are we being tempted to stay in a safe past rather than to venture into the risky present? Any process of change can arouse anxieties and reveal the insecurities of the people who are concerned in it.

Imagine yourself invited once more to an annual dinner and discovering that you had not noticed, or had not been informed that this year 'evening dress' was expected. Smart though your lounge suit may be, your embarrassment and unpreparedness for this situation severely limit your ability to enjoy the celebration, and you may well feel cheated because of your unfulfilled expectation. You are likely to be cautious about attending that particular event again.

Much the same feelings may detract from the celebration of a congregation which having come to worship within an expected routine suddenly find an 'experimental' service thrust upon them. Despite their charity there will be those in the congregation who will feel they have been treated with less than proper dignity, and such inconsiderate action on the part of the preacher will not encourage sympathy for the idea of experiment. It will in fact prevent him from achieving his primary objective—creating the conditions for the *congregation* to celebrate.

The preacher should share his thoughts on experiments with the leaders of the church and with the people so far as is possible, so that they can prepare themselves in mind and attitude for the experiment, and know that their own co-operation and contribution are valued. The preacher who seeks this co-operation will rarely be refused it.[7]

(a) The experiment is born in a concern

An experiment in worship is not created by a preacher saying to himself, 'Next Sunday I'll try an experimental service at Ebenezer'—any more than a great hymn is likely to result from a man saying 'I think I'll try writing a new hymn this morning.' Like great hymns which set the people singing, a worthy experiment in worship is born in a concern which cannot find adequate expression in any existing form. It is this integrity of concern which distinguishes true experiment in worship from mere gimmickry.

(b) The search for a method

Suppose a preacher is disturbed by the thought that dedication seems to take place too easily and formally in the habitual forms of worship. How can he order worship so that dedication becomes more meaningful? He broods on the problem. Perhaps the reason for this situation is that the distinctive character of God is not seen clearly enough; or that the contrast of this character against the

[7] See also chapter 7, pp. 129–30.

contemporary background of events and attitudes needs to be brought out. How can this be done? The sermon can become visibly a dialogue between two points of view, so that the congregation might see more clearly what their committal to God means. Or the conflict can be revealed by contrasting readings from scripture and daily newspapers. In this way the preacher seeks his method.

(c) *The building of an order*

Concern having given birth to method, what ordering of worship will best carry this method? If the sermon becomes a dialogue, is it going to be most helpful in one, two or three stages? The appropriate praise, thanksgiving, intercession, petition and dedication may follow in a meditation after each section; two or three of the hymns can be chosen to provide for worship needs which the limitations of this theme and method cannot include.

(d) *Principles of experiments in worship*

1. Recollect that worship is the *people's celebration of God*. This will help us to guard against some of the temptations peculiar to preparing experiments in services. 'We preach not ourselves, but Christ Jesus as Lord, and ourselves your servants for his sake,' said Paul. This is true for preaching and for the experimental elements you may be introducing. Consider the motive for your experiment, and see that you are not trying to debase worship into an entertainment or a technique of persuasion.

2. Do not let preoccupation with your theme exclude from the liturgy the continual daily needs of your congregation. The experimental event should not become more important than the grief of a bereaved wife, the anxieties of a father of a broken home, the delight of a couple in church for the first time after the arrival of their firstborn, the insecurity of the middle-aged executive wondering how

he can hold his job with all the bright young ambitious men pressing behind him. Some or all of these may be in the congregation. Ensure that there is opportunity for the people to 'make prayers and supplications, and to give thanks for all men'—a place to ask the good Lord to comfort and succour 'all who in this transitory life are in trouble, sorrow, need, sickness or any other adversity'.

3. Understand the place of your experiment in the whole pattern of that congregation's services. The inevitable debate on 'Experiment versus Tradition' can often be resolved if preacher and Leaders see a compromise in terms of *change within a routine*. Experiments take their place within an existing routine of (say) communion, baptism and parade services.

4. Make an opportunity to explain the changes in the order of worship and the reason for them. This can be done before the service begins or after an opening devotional section. The people will know that *they* are not just 'objects' on which you are practising your bright ideas, but friends invited to share a celebration. Avoid giving too much explanation, or your congregation will be saying 'Why doesn't he stop talking and get on with it?' A concise, well-prepared statement is called for, with duplicated copies of the order of worship to help those whose hearing is not good, and those who may arrive late.

5. Experiment must be grounded in the given real situation, not an ideal imaginary one. Suppose I find it necessary for the congregation to share some form of group work in the course of the service. However laudable my intention may be, it will still be useless to impose this on a congregation of a scattering of elderly people, some sixty in all in a church seating 500, fitted with pews, and where heating is only adequate along the back rows! Take account of the given conditions, not only to avoid practical difficulties, but to take advantage of any resources provided

by that situation. A balcony may be useful, as may three aisles, or moveable communion furniture. The congregation may be elderly, but a wealth of experience and conviction and skills may be available in it.

6. Experiment demands evaluation. Experiments in worship need to be assessed so that their value may be understood in the continuing liturgical experience of the church. Was the method successful? Did the service prove a real celebration? Was it too long, too short—if so, why? Did it in fact provide a means of release for any particular group, or a source of dissatisfaction for any others? Could it have been improved, and what insights are worth trying again? Did the service promote any desire for action, and if so how is it to be followed up?

Shrewdness and honesty in asking these questions will help to avoid the danger of soliciting congratulations. Why not bring the service into the forum of the Local Preachers' Meeting?

Example of an experimental service—a service created by a group

At a time when the organization Shelter was making a national appeal, a housegroup belonging to a church in a new town felt that this concern should find expression in the church's liturgy. The Leaders' Meeting had already agreed on the possibility of house groups being involved in leading worship.

For some time the group brooded on various aspects of homelessness, making use of a report produced by a neighbouring Congregational church on local housing needs. What did homelessness mean to an evicted family, to the aged or lonely? What was the effect of inadequate housing on health and education? What people were striving to meet these needs and how? The group was aware of a common underlying theme emerging—housing problems and concern about them are a direct expression of human faith.

The group then discussed the method, which was to present a number of these life situations, followed in each case by a short scripture reading which would suggest the Christian focus on that situation.

Tasks were allocated to various group members: some had to follow up certain case-histories and arrange them for presentation: another couple were asked to search out a list of hymns which might prove appropriate for such a service: a local preacher in the group was asked to prepare intercessions, based on concerns that had been voiced in discussion. Someone else was asked to tape-record interviews with two pioneers of local housing projects.

Seven people shared in the leadership of the service, all of whom had probably learned a little more of what the task of celebration involves. Worship was demonstrated as a congregational activity, shown to be integrated with daily life, and seen to call for practical service.

Hymn 270
Prayer
Junior choir
Hymn 845 (then children leave for Junior Church)
Notices and explanation of service
Lessons (Theme—hospitality)
       1 Kings 17:10–16
       Hebrews 13:1–16
Hymn 911
'Sermon' Narrative of experience of evicted mother and children who discovered earlier promises of hospitality empty.
       Matt. 21:28–31a
       Readings from *Christian Action* (Winter '66 pp. 5 and 6) on housing, health and education.
       James 2:15–17

What can one man do? Recorded interviews.
   Matthew 17:20

A last-minute introduction—of a newspaper report of the death of Gladys Aylward in her work of providing homes for Chinese Children.

   John 15:13

Our home in Christ (G. K. Chesterton, *House of Christmas*).

Intercessions, using words of 891 in responses
Offering
Thanksgiving and dedication
Hymn 390

This service was not beyond improvement, and thoughtful readers will already have more appropriate hymns and readings to suggest. The service was a little too long. The aim could have been more simplified. But it was a sign of how God is present to the Christian community; in a fresh way it was the celebration of his people.

V   In Celebration there is re-creation

Although the primary aim of worship is to celebrate God, not meet our own clamant needs, there is no doubt that often our deep needs *are* met. In any celebration influential memories are aroused, relationships re-created, deep emotions set free. The grace of our family life is recognized afresh, and perhaps new pledges are made, private and public, to maintain the family bonds in good repair.

So the worship of the family of God can become the ground of change and re-creation. We struggle to interpret our life in the life of the Holy Spirit, we affirm his presence as he is disclosed to us, and in dedication we identify our lives with his. God is working in us that which is well pleasing in his sight.

Note on gesture and posture in worship

Actions can speak as loudly as words, as the impact of films and television confirms. Men encountered truth through prophetic, symbolic action (Ahijah tearing his robe, 1 Kings 11:30; David pouring out the water from the well at Bethlehem, 2 Sam. 23:16) and especially through the action of Jesus in accepting crucifixion ('I, if I be lifted up . . .') and in breaking the bread ('This is my body given for you . . .'). Many a preacher uses dramatic action or visual aids when leading the worship of young people.

On the other hand it is true that overposturing and flamboyant gestures, if not ridiculous, may prove offensive to the congregation, drawing attention to the preacher himself, and raising questions about his motivation. So we avoid ostentatious prayer before the sermon and guard against similar undesirable exhibitionist tendencies.

The preacher, as the servant of the celebration, can make use of the church in the action of worship, moving from the lectern (for the lessons) to the pulpit (for the sermon) and to the Communion Table (saying prayers with the people rather than over against them), and saying the Benediction from there. In the dedication of the offering, it may be helpful to encourage the congregation to stand, thus reminding them that the dedication is the dedication of their own lives.

What posture are we to expect from our people when in prayer? Many feel that it is right and proper to kneel, expressing our humility before God. Others can best say their prayers in a relaxed sitting position. The latter has been jocularly described as the non-conformist crouch, but there is often no option for the former in Methodist churches (for there are usually no hassocks, no adequate room to kneel in the pews, and to kneel is to draw attention to oneself). All that we can reasonably ask for is freedom in our churches to practise that which we find to be most helpful.

Gestures and symbolic religious actions should be simple, few, and understandable. Multiplication of these can have the effect of overemphasizing the distinction between regular worshipper and visitor in a way that is unhelpful if not alienating to strangers.

Useful Books

Prayers of Life—Michel Quoist (Gill & Son 1963)
Worship and Preaching—Morrow, Billington and Bates (Epworth 1967)

5. Readings, Prayers and Hymns

David Blatherwick

Readings—the choice

As preachers we must recognize the conflict between our desire to use familiar material and our congregation's need for varied and comprehensive teaching. The lay preacher in particular will find it difficult to plan a different service for each Sunday, but we must all accept some challenge to widen our knowledge and increase our ability to speak with assurance on the major Christian themes.

The introduction in some places of Family Worship and the integrated British Lessons Council Sunday School syllabus has put additional pressure on the preacher to bear his congregation's needs in mind. Wherever children share in hymns, prayers and (sometimes) readings before going into their Sunday School classes, the worship must l e related to the lesson which is to follow. (Direct consultation between preachers and Sunday School staff is most desirable, but where this is not possible the preacher can still keep himself informed through a copy of the lesson notes or the explanatory booklet *Experience and Faith*.)

Sometimes experiments are made in 'group preaching'.[1] Three or four preachers can plan a series of services leading up to Christmas or Easter, or dealing with certain aspects

[1] See chapter 9, p. 156.

of our faith. In this way some of the disadvantages of having different preachers each Sunday can be overcome, but it should always be done in consultation with the church or churches concerned.

But above all, every preacher should consider seriously the use of the Methodist Lectionary. Use of the suggested theme, with prayer and readings, for each Sunday of the year will help to ensure that congregations receive varied and yet comprehensive teaching from the pulpit. It demands careful preparation—planning ahead. It will be made very much simpler if there is a preachers' discussion group in which difficulties can be discussed. But over a period of years, as he reads more widely and gains in experience, the preacher will find little difficulty in planning his services on the basis of the Lectionary and both he and his congregations will reap the benefit.

The readings themselves

It is the habit of most Methodist preachers to have two Bible readings, each at a set point in the service. Some preachers reduce the number to one—'in order to save time'. But now the Lectionary and *The Sunday Service* suggest the use of three, with a Psalm to be used in addition (either chanted or read by preacher and congregation).

The new suggestions are logical. The Psalms are by nature songs rather than readings and should be treated as such, and there is a certain completeness about using the three main sections of Scripture in one service—the Old Testament preparation for Christ, the apostolic witness to Christ, and the life and teaching of Christ himself. But why limit ourselves to two or three readings? Why not have more and why stop at the end of the Biblical narrative?

Taking the last point first, we need to remember that the purpose of the Bible readings is to anchor the Church's faith and worship in its historical beginnings and to rejoice in the mighty acts and promises of God recounted for us in the Bible. It is therefore undesirable to include material at this point of the service which would obscure the teaching of the Bible or appear to be a substitute for it. But with this reservation there is no reason why brief quotations from Christian thinkers, past and present, nor even poetry or other literature, should not be used to illuminate a theme which is obviously being traced out with reference to Scripture.

Some attempts to gather together suitable readings from non-biblical sources have been made recently. Two examples are *Word Alive* by M. Banyard and *Words for Worship* by C. Campling and M. Davies. Religious poetry will be found in *Let there be God* by T. H. Parker and F. Teskey and *God's Trombones* by J. W. Johnson, as well as in the poetry of Sidney Carter. But ultimately the preacher's source must be his own reading of religious and secular literature. He must avoid sensationalism and obscurity and undue length, but above all he must believe in what he is reading. Then he may find that he can lead his congregation to a deeper understanding of the Biblical message.

Bible readings can also be obscure and too long!

The length of our readings will be determined by what we are reading, but we should remember that two short readings are usually more effective than one long one and that 10 to 15 verses should usually be the maximum from any one passage. It may be right sometimes to exceed that limit, but on the other hand we should not be afraid to omit verses, especially where the extra material is obscure or unnecessary to our point and where the basic meaning is not altered by the omission. When the material relevant to our theme is contained in one saying or a brief story, it is worth experimenting with a chain of short readings which can be read one after the other—an obvious example would be a collection of sayings and parables about the kingdom of God.

We need to practise our reading before we enter the pulpit so that we know exactly how to convey the meaning and the feeling of the passage. In order to draw the congregation into the act of worship, we should encourage capable people to read for us. To add variety and interest, two or three readers can share a reading, especially where a chain of quotations is being used. Nor should we be afraid of dramatizing the Bible or using a popular re-telling of a familiar story (e.g. *Stories from the Bible* by David Kossoff or *Children's Bible Stories* by D. A. Cramer-Schaap) if the occasion demands it.

Readings should be introduced simply. If there is anything unusual about the presentation, the congregation should be told what to expect. If a large number of short readings is to be used, a general introduction is preferable to an attempt to give all the references. Pompous introductions ('Here beginneth . . .', etc.) should be avoided—a simple announcement like 'The gospel reading is from Mark chapter 2, beginning at verse 13' is quite enough.

Our aim should be to make all readings self-explanatory or capable of being understood with the minimum of comment—long explanations belong to the sermon. When introductory comments are required they should be limited to presenting the main characters or setting the passage against its historical background. In the same way, there should be no need for any comment at the end. Some preachers feel that 'Here ends the lesson' or 'Thanks be to God' is appropriate, but longer sentences, especially 'May the Lord add his blessing to the reading of his Word', should be avoided (is not the Bible reading itself God's blessing—assuming that it has been suitably chosen and adequately read?).

Finally, we should seek the translation of the Bible which is simplest for the congregation to understand and for us to read. We shall probably not find complete satisfaction in any one version, but will keep two or three close at hand. Whereas previous generations of preachers had limited choice outside the Authorized and Revised Versions, we must now consider seriously the claims of the *New English Bible*, the *Jerusalem Bible* and the Revised Standard Version—and, for the New Testament alone, J. B. Phillips, *Good News for Modern Man* and, on occasions, the lively paraphrase of key passages found in Alan Dale's *New World*. Resistance to new translations is rapidly disappearing, and although we should recognize that different translations sometimes imply a difference of theological outlook, we should not be afraid of making use of the greater simplicity, liveliness and attractiveness of the modern versions.

Prayers—a contemporary style

With regard to prayers, we must again plead for the simplest and most effective language. Unfortunately the revision of liturgical language is not as far advanced as the re-translation of the Bible, but we can find some guidelines in *Contemporary Prayers for Public Worship* (ed. C. Micklem), *Worship for Today* (ed. R. G. Jones) and some of the prayer books of William Barclay. (The remarkable style of *Prayers of Life* by M. Quoist and *Are you running with me, Jesus?* by M. Boyd is on the whole suited to private meditation or public reading rather than leading corporate prayer.)

The most obvious problem in modernizing liturgical language is the traditional 'Thee' and 'Thou' used in addressing God. First, it creates difficulties of construction and pronunciation, especially for the beginner. Secondly, it is disturbing to the stranger in worship, especially to young people. On the other hand, the regular churchgoer may object to 'You' (even the New English Bible translators objected to this familiarity) and we cannot ignore the fact that 'Thee' and 'Thou' will still appear in the Lord's Prayer, some readings and the hymns. Nevertheless it seems to have been the practice of Jesus to address God with extreme familiarity ('Abba, Father'—Mark 14:36) and a sense of intimacy with God was one of the hallmarks of the early Christian experience (Romans 8:15; Galatians 4:4). It would therefore seem desirable to move steadily in the direction of the more natural speech, while recognizing the ability of many to express modern thoughts in the older style (e.g. *One Man's Prayers* by G. Appleton).

But it is not enough to modernize the way in which we address God. If we really wish to offer prayer in a contemporary style we must pay attention to the content of our prayers. We cannot carry over into the twentieth century the thought-forms of an earlier age, but must allow our prayers to grow out of our own understanding of our faith and the world in which we live. This means in particular (although we recognize that many different opinions are sincerely held on these matters):

(a) Our prayers should reflect a contemporary understanding of God. This does not mean that we should use technical theological language in prayers, nor that we should use prayer to press home our particular ideas, but simply that we should be alive to the ways in which people's thoughts are changing.

(b) Our prayers should reflect a contemporary understanding of the Church. Our growing sense of the Church as God's community giving itself in service to mankind should find expression in our prayers.

(c) Our prayers should reflect a contemporary understanding of the world's needs. This means in the first place that we cannot ignore questions of world poverty, illiteracy, disease, war and peace, racial integration—these are some of the fundamental issues of our time which must be the burden of prayer. In the second place it means that we must see our work and prayer alongside that of other nations, other religions and ideologies, and that our prayers should reflect a healthy and right attitude towards the whole family of man.

We should conclude our prayers with a simple phrase like 'through Jesus Christ our Lord'. The use of high-sounding, flattering words is out of place in Christian prayer, as much at the conclusion as at the beginning. Phrases like 'if it be thy will' should be avoided because they give the picture of a capricious God. A quick glance through a prayer book will suggest other suitable expressions and it is worth noting that some modern writers simply put *Amen* at the end of their request.

It is perhaps strange that the Hebrew word *Amen* should have been used throughout the history of the Church at the conclusion of prayers, but there is no obvious alternative. If we remember that it represents a confident 'It shall be so' (literally 'Truly!') or even an aggressive 'We shall make it so' (certainly not a weak, submissive 'Let it be so'), we shall see the importance of asking the congregation to join wholeheartedly in this response—we shall also see the importance of making our prayers the expression of the heartfelt desires of our congregation.

Leading the congregation in prayer

(a) *Written or Extempore Prayer*

Apart from the books of contemporary prayers mentioned in the last section, the preacher has a vast array of traditional prayer books available to him as he prepares for worship. The *Book of Offices* and *The Sunday Service* remind us of our Methodist tradition of written prayers. The *Book of Common Worship* (and equally useful Supplement) of the Church of South India will offer the lay preacher a much wider range of written prayers, as will anthologies like *Parish Prayers* by F. Colquhoun.

The written prayer has obvious attractions for the beginner, but it is not only beginners who will make use of such prayers. Many preachers prefer the traditional prayers of the Church, partly because their style and appropriateness appeals to them, partly because they know they are appreciated by many members of their congregations.

Three warnings might perhaps be given:

(1) Do not gabble written prayers or read them in such a way that it is difficult for the congregation to follow.

(2) Do not use traditional prayers where the language is obscure or the theology unacceptable.

(3) Avoid tinkering about with the language. It is usually better to write a new prayer in your own style than to attempt to 'modernize' an older one.

Most preachers will in addition want the freedom to compose their own prayers. These can be written out beforehand and read carefully in the service or they can be prepared in the mind or even, on occasions, produced spontaneously (what is traditionally called 'extempore prayer'). All preachers should make experiments in spontaneous prayer because they are frequently confronted with unexpected situations and must try to express the congregation's concerns in their prayers. But it is in fact very difficult to compose prayers 'standing on our feet' unless we reproduce one basic pattern, often in almost exactly the same words, time after time. Therefore:

(1) Give thought beforehand. Plan the prayer in your mind so that before you begin to speak you know what you wish to say (and what there is no time to say).

(2) Do not ramble (extempore prayers sometimes sound like an introduction to theology or a spiritual 'Cook's tour of the world').

(3) If we are tempted to regard prayer as an opportunity to show off our skill, we should be warned by Paul, dealing with a different but related issue, 'The language of ecstasy is good for the speaker himself, but it is prophecy (i.e. speech whose meaning is plain) that builds up a Christian community' (1 Corinthians 14:4).

(b) Allowing the congregation to participate

Our aim in leading prayer should be to enable the congregation to pray. We should encourage the congregation to feel that they can join in:

(1) By the use of silence. A period of silence may be given (no more than two minutes or until the congregation becomes restless) but the congregation can also be encouraged to pray their own prayers if there are helpful pauses in the prayers or if bidding prayers are used (i.e. 'Let us pray for . . .'—a good example is the prayer of intercession in *The Sunday Service*).

(2) The congregation may be asked to suggest topics for prayer or they may be invited to offer their own brief prayers during a period of 'open prayer'. Alternatively, if the preacher feels that the congregation would be shy, he can ask certain members beforehand to offer prayer at this point of the service.

(3) Certain written prayers can be said together. Many hymn books have the General Confession and General Thanksgiving printed on the inside covers. Some contain the *Book of Offices*. All contain Psalms and Canticles and hymns which can be used as congregational prayers.

(4) Responsive prayers can be used. Obvious sources are *The Sunday Service* and the *Book of Offices* (e.g. the prayers of adoration, thanksgiving and confession in the

Covenant Service) and many churches will have copies of these for the congregation. But as long as the preacher announces the response clearly and as long as it is clear where the response should be made, this form of prayer can be used even when the congregation does not have the words. (Here there is an obvious advantage when the response is preceded by a 'versicle' spoken by the preacher, as in the traditional 'Lord hear our prayer' and response 'And let our cry come unto thee'. More attractive examples will be found in the Church of South India litany which begins 'For the peace that is from above, and for the salvation of our souls—Let us pray to the Lord'—Response 'Lord have mercy' (or alternatively 'The Lord hears our prayer'—see *The Book of Common Worship*, p. 12), and in *The Sunday Service*, Versicle 'Lord in your mercy'—Response 'Hear our prayer'.

Certain types of prayer

It is possible for all the basic elements of worship (adoration, confession, etc.)[2] to be the subject of prayer, just as it is possible for any of these aspects to be included in the service through a hymn, a reading, preacher's comment or sermon. There is therefore no simple answer to the question 'What themes should be covered by the prayers?' except the apparent evasion 'It all depends on how you have planned the service'.

Nevertheless certain points ought to be brought to the beginner's notice.

1 Adoration

Adoration (i.e. sheer wonder at the greatness and goodness of God) is not so much one theme for prayer as an

[2] See chapter 1, pp. 20–28. This section should be related to the orders of service on pp. 68–9.

atmosphere that should pervade the whole act of worship. The 'doxology' at the end of the Lord's Prayer ('For thine is the kingdom . . .') reminds us that the simplest Jewish prayer would contain an ascription of glory to God. But it is traditional that we should introduce an element of adoration at the beginning of the service in the choice of our first hymn or as part of the content of our opening prayer.

2 Prayers of Invocation

Sometimes brief prayers of invocation or aspiration (after the fashion of the Lectionary 'Collects') are more suitable as an introduction to worship than the traditional prayers of adoration and confession. These prayers will reflect the theme of the service, ask God's blessing on the worship or be a realization of God's presence. The brevity and simplicity of this type of prayer is particularly valuable when children are present.

3 Confession

Prayers of confession should always be used in the light of the assurance of God's forgiveness. We may remind the congregation of God's love before the prayer or we may give an assurance of his forgiveness at the close (e.g. *The Sunday Service, Worship for Today* pp. 18, 25, 28, 57, 61, and the Declaration of Forgiveness in the order on pp. 68–9).

Secondly, we should bear in mind, not simply that children will find this aspect of prayer difficult to accept, but that even adults feel that we spread gloom and despondency by the type of prayers we use.

Thirdly, we might look carefully at the wide range of prayers of confession covered by the references to *Worship for Today*—some prayers are quite general, some are specific (and we should alternate between the two), and some prayers concentrate on 'what we have done and left undone', while others refer to a sense of dis-ease and a feeling of complicity in the inhumanity of so much contemporary life (both surely have their place).

4 *Thanksgiving and Adoration*

In worship we gather together to celebrate 'the mighty acts of God' in Creation and Redemption. We do this in the Bible readings and sermon, but at this point of the service, in response to the Ministry of the Word, we give thanks in prayer for our creation and for the life, death and resurrection of Jesus. Any thanksgiving for other gifts we have received should be set in the context of this offering of thanks for the supreme gift.

This part of worship is seen in the Communion Service in 'The Great Prayer of Thanksgiving (see p. 12 of *The Sunday Service*). A prayer of Thanksgiving such as this should be included in every complete act of Christian worship. (There is an example for a Preaching Service—where there is no Communion—on pp. 22–3 of *The Sunday Service*.)

Thanksgiving and adoration come close to one another at this point and in the Communion Service the prayer o thanksgiving leads into the 'Sanctus' ('Holy, holy, holy . . .'). The note of adoration with which the service began can be taken up again and a prayer which is suitable for congregational use, like the Sanctus, can be used here if it has not already been used at the beginning.

5 *Intercessions*

Concern for our Christian brothers and for the world in which we live lies at the heart of our Christian life. Unfortunately this is rarely expressed adequately in worship, especially in the Free Churches. A service which contains no prayers of intercession at all is hardly Christian, and a service where the prayers are for the congregation, its family and friends, even for the wider Christian family, but not for the world at large, is severely distorted. In 1 Timothy 2:1-3 we are exhorted to pray for all in need, including pagan tyrants. In the Lord's Prayer we seek the coming of God's kingdom. Intercession must therefore be taken seriously by all Christians.

(*a*) The preacher can help the congregation to pray realistically for their own church and for those in need in the locality by referring to particular people, organizations and causes before the prayer. (This will perhaps save us from the prayer which begins 'Lord, you know that Mrs Jones has been very ill. . . .' It will also help to keep the congregation informed about their church and neighbourhood.)

(*b*) The preacher can help the congregation to pray for the wider Church. This will require a knowledge of the work of Methodism at district and national level, knowledge of the needs of other Christian communities and of the World Church. (*Praying for the World Church* and other publications of the Missionary Society and the World Council of Churches will help here.)

(*c*) The preacher can help the congregation to pray for the needs of the wider community—for social and political concerns, national and international affairs, for a true understanding of other races, nations, religions and ideologies. (Here our guides are the daily press and religious and secular weeklies.)

These three observations should be enough to remind the preacher that he cannot hope to cover the needs of the world in one act of prayer! Perhaps it has also indicated that as much preparation (selecting themes, gathering correct information, etc.) goes into helpful prayers as into helpful sermons.

6 Petition

We should have no fear, as long as we avoid the dangers

of excessive self-concern, about leading a congregation to pray for itself, either as a community or as individuals. In fact, it is as we see ourselves as a serving community that we become most conscious of our inadequacies and our need of God's help and guidance.

7 *Dedication*

The congregation must sense the close link between worship, the life of the church and everyday life. In the collection prayer we offer ourselves in the service of God, but this prayer should be brief to be effective. We need therefore to provide a further opportunity for the offering to God of our act of worship, the ongoing life of the church and ourselves during the week. This can be achieved in a simple prayer and perhaps a time of silence.

8 *The Lord's Prayer*

Although it is common to repeat the Lord's Prayer at the close of the so-called 'first prayer', this is not necessarily its most suitable position. As the prayer which sums up the basic desire of the Christian worshipper it can belong at the beginning of worship with suitable, brief preliminary prayer, or it can be used equally aptly at the close of prayers of intercession and dedication later in the service. (We should observe that attempts have been made, and are still being made, to re-translate the Lord's Prayer, but so far they have met with considerable opposition. For a fuller understanding of the prayer we should turn to our New Testament textbooks and commentaries.)

Hymns—words and tunes

Despite recent interest in modern hymns, the preacher is on the whole severely restricted in choosing hymns for congregational singing. A number of churches will have bought *Hymns and Songs*, but few will be prepared to go to the expense of providing a wider selection of modern hymns for the congregation. So long as the organist and choir are co-operative the preacher will be able to use new tunes to old hymns, but the real task of introducing modern hymns, words and music, into our worship must still be left to the choir or individuals who are interested in exploring the growing mass of suitable material.

Yet for many preachers interest in modern hymn-writing is academic. Their problem is whether there will be an organist at all or whether the congregation will be large enough for there to be any joy in singing. For them it is sometimes preferable to have no music and to sing un-accompanied rather than have the singing made difficult by an inadequate organist or pianist.

Even in larger churches there is a need for a revival of the enjoyment of singing. This can sometimes be achieved through the encouragement of small groups to explore the hymn book and modern supplements. But these groups will only be able to help the whole congregation if preach-ers are prepared to consult with them in planning services. Although (in Methodist churches at least) the choice of hymns is usually left to the preacher, he cannot exercise his right to choose as though only his opinion matters. What is required is a working relationship between the preacher and the congregation, especially stewards, organ-ist, choirmaster and any others concerned with the church's worship.

Much of the worry of choosing hymns (a job which is often left to the last minute and should not be!) can be removed by careful preparatory work. The *Methodist Hymn Book* and the supplement contain over 1,050 hymns, the majority of which are unknown to our congre-gations and many of which we would have no wish to use even if the tunes were familiar. In order to get to know the hymn books and to separate the good from the bad, we should look through each hymn carefully and make a note of those hymns which we feel are suitable for use.

In the first place we should select hymns for their words. As with prayers we should look for language that is simple and clear. We should look for thoughts that are specifically Christian rather than vaguely religious. We should be wary of hymns steeped in a Biblical language that our congregations would not understand (though on certain occasions and with certain congregations we may feel we can experiment with more difficult hymns). We should never choose hymns whose theology we cannot accept (though on occasions we shall have to let our congregations choose them!). Other valuable points to bear in mind in looking at the hymn book can be found in A. S. Gregory's article in *Preacher's Handbook, No. 11*, chapter 10.

When we have a provisional selection of hymns, we should enlist the support of a musical friend or group of singers in order to consider the tunes. Often a good hymn is destroyed by a bad tune and it is necessary to seek a better one. Sometimes a hymn about which we are doubtful is improved by the tune. Whether the preacher is musical or not he should develop a keen sense of which hymns are singable and also a sense of the size of congregation for which they are suitable.

It is much simpler to work from a list of about 250 hymns (with a separate list for Christmas, Easter, etc.), with notes about tunes and suitability, than to work from the index to the whole hymn book, and the result will probably be a wider range of hymns than would normally be achieved. (It is of course necessary to keep the notes up to date and to revise the list from time to time in the light of bitter experience and a growing understanding of theology and hymnody.) It is then simple to keep a record of the hymns we choose and to avoid choosing certain hymns too frequently.

In detailed preparation for a service:

(1) Select hymns appropriate to the season of the Church Year and/or to the theme of the service, or appropriate to the points of the service at which they will be used.

(2) Provide variety in the hymns. Have both long and short, lively and meditative. Vary the metre—it is not good to have too many hymns in the same style. Vary the theme —it is not good to belabour one theme in all the hymns. Also vary the authors—use the full range of Christian hymns (i.e. not all Charles Wesley!).

(3) Value especially those hymns which are objective and express joy, adoration, thanks, confidence in the faith. These are usually more suitable for congregational singing than the highly introspective, emotional hymns.

(4) Do not include too many unusual or unknown hymns in one service. Congregations will usually try to sing a new hymn if they are encouraged to do so by a word of explanation, but it is rarely wise to introduce more than one new tune in each service.[3]

(5) Remember that there is no divine command that we should have five hymns in a service. Be prepared to vary the pattern and be ready to introduce a note of modernity into the service through the choir, a group or a soloist (so long as it is planned carefully in advance).

[3] With regard to announcing hymns we should avoid the habit of giving the number twice, reading four or more lines of the first verse and then repeating the number. This is appropriate perhaps for outdoor services and churches with no hymn board, but is usually unnecessary. So long as the organist knows what to expect, a clear announcement of the number and perhaps the first line should be enough.

In Church

Useful Books

READINGS

Experience and Faith, A Christian Education Syllabus—produced on behalf of the British Lessons Council, by Methodist Youth Dept. and others.

Collects, Lessons and Psalms—New Lectionary of the Methodist Church (Methodist Publishing House)

Word Alive—M. Banyard (Galliard 1969)

Words for Worship—C. Campling and M. Davies (Edward Arnold 1969)

Let there be God—ed. T. H. Parker and F. Teskey (R.E.P. 1968)

God's Trombones—J. W. Johnson (George Allen & Unwin 1963)

Nothing Fixed or Final and other works of Sidney Carter (Galliard 1969)

Stories from the Bible—D. Kossoff (Collins 1968)

Children's Bible Stories—D. A. Cramer-Schaap (Nelson 1964)

New World: The heart of the New Testament in Plain English—A. T. Dale (Oxford University Press 1967)

The Local Preacher Reads his Lessons (Local Preachers' Department Pamphlet)

PRAYERS

Contemporary Prayers for Public Worship—ed. C. Micklem (S.C.M. Press 1967)

More Contemporary Prayers—ed. C. Micklem (S.C.M. Press 1970)

Worship for Today—ed. R. Jones (Epworth 1968)

Prayers of Life—M. Quoist (Gill and Son, 1st ed. 1963)

Are you running with me, Jesus?—M. Boyd (S.C.M. Press/Heinemann 1967)

One Man's Prayers—G. Appleton (S.P.C.K. 1967)

The Sunday Service and *The Book of Offices* (Methodist Publishing House)

The Book of Common Worship of the Church of South India (Oxford University Press 1963) and Supplement

Parish Prayers—F. Colquhoun (Hodder and Stoughton 1967)

Orders and Prayers for Church Worship—E. A. Payne and S. Winward (Carey Kingsgate Press 1962)

A Manual for Ministers (Independent Press)

Praying for the World Church (Methodist Missionary Society and Local Preachers' Department)

The Local Preacher Leads in Prayer (Local Preachers' Department Pamphlet)

HYMNS

Hymns and Songs, Supplement to the Methodist Hymn Book (Methodist Publishing House)

100 Hymns, Supplement to *Hymns Ancient & Modern*

Sing True—ed. Colin Hodgetts (R.E.P. 1969)

Faith, Folk and Clarity (1967)

Faith, Folk and Nativity (1968)

Faith, Folk and Festivity (1969)

    —ed. P. Smith (Galliard)

New Songs for the Church 1 and 2—ed. R. Barrett—Ayres and E. Routley (Galliard 1969)

20th Century Hymn Book Supplement and other publications of the 20th Century Church Light Music Group (Josef Weinberger Ltd)

Preachers Handbook No. 11—ed. John Stacey (Epworth 1969)

The Local Preacher Chooses his Hymns (Local Preachers' Department Pamphlet)

6. Young People at Worship

James B. Bates

I The approach to young people

WHEN we baptize children we welcome them into the family of the church. From their earliest years they belong to the church and share in its life as far as they are able. In Sunday School they learn about their heritage and worship in a way suited to their experience and needs, but it is equally important that they share in the worship of the church so that they become aware of the community to which they belong. Only in this way can their confirmation of membership become real.

In helping the children to share in worship the preacher has a key role, but he must never think of himself in isolation. He is working with the congregation and the Sunday School. Consultation, therefore, is essential. Every preacher should, by visiting or discussion, or even by a telephone call to the Superintendent, find out what is happening in the Sunday School and learn all he can from those whose special responsibility is that of understanding and helping children.

In the field of education a great deal of research has been carried out into the nature of children's religious experience, and a number of relevant books are listed in the bibliography at the end of this chapter.

II The child's religious experience

(*a*) *Has its roots in personal relationships.* It is within the family that a child discovers his own identity and the basic relationships with others on which his whole personal life is built. Without the security of home the child does not develop freely, and without the experience of parental love the love of God is almost impossible to understand (at best it is only learned by compensatory experiences). The child senses very quickly whether he is welcome or not when he is introduced into wider social groups, and attitudes to the church are formed by the way in which the adult congregation considers his needs and his importance. Children do not want condescension and fussing, but they do need to be understood and to be able to share in what is happening. They want to feel they belong, and that the community they belong to is a happy one. They need also to feel that what they share in is important, both to them and the adults. The atmosphere of a service is important to a child, he is sensitive to the spirit in which it is led and shared.

(*b*) *Expresses itself in wonder at life.* Most of us can recall childhood memories with pleasure, there was an intensity about our experiences of the world which is seldom, if ever, equalled in later life. Wonder comes naturally to children, they are at the same time baffled, delighted and fascinated by a thousand things which we regard as commonplace and take for granted. Wonder lies at the basis of worship, and it is out of our response to life itself that our religious experience comes. Worship, therefore, should be closely related to direct experiences of life. The themes of our service, the choice of our hymns, the wording of our prayers will be guided by this. It is out of their experience of the goodness of life that they come to trust in the goodness of God, and it is in worship that they should find the bridge.

(*c*) *Is a quest for meaning*. Wonder provokes enquiry and the exploration of experience is essential to the religious development. This means that the teacher who is able to help a child personally in his quest is better placed than the preacher. The preacher, however, in conducting worship is well placed to help children in their religious understanding. Worship provokes enquiry, and through this the child can discover the meaning of the faith and practice of the church. Worship must, therefore, be meaningful and its meaning made clear. Elaborate explanations are not possible or needed, but the preacher must say 'what' is being done and indicate 'why' in clear and simple terms. It goes without saying that he will then do what he says. In this way he will guide the child along the right lines of enquiry.

(*d*) *Finds expression in activity*. Children worship and learn by doing, but so much of our adult worship is passive. Apart from singing hymns we do little but listen. Children find listening for anything more than a minute or two a burden. In school they learn by activities and become involved and interested by doing things. So the preacher must strictly limit the length of time in which he expects the children to listen and think out ways in which they can be active in the worship. This is not easy in a mixed congregation, but short varied acts will help to dispel boredom and excite interest.

(*e*) Finally, it should be remembered that children think literally and learn by direct experience. Therefore we should avoid abstract and metaphorical language, keeping to topics which are well within their range of experience. God will become real for them in so far as he is closely related to what they know, and described in terms they can understand. Later, a child will qualify such terms (e.g. Father) but if they are the right terms then he will not have been misled or confused.

III   The problems and opportunities

The problems which come to the preacher who is leading worship where children are present are so many that some feel it is better for all concerned if children worship on their own. While few would advocate that children sit through the whole of an adult service, they need to share with adults in worship if they are to realize their place within the family of the church. There are problems, but in facing them the preacher can come to a new understanding of his role which can help everyone.

(*a*) *The children are of all ages* and their understanding will be at different levels. For the youngest most of what we say will be quite meaningless, but where understanding separates, atmosphere unites. Long before they can grasp ideas intellectually children sense reality and can enjoy being part of a congregation which worships as a family. Therefore in leading worship in such a way that the congregation can respond as a whole the preacher is helping the child to worship.

Yet children can understand, and want to, so the preacher must strive for clarity and simplicity, avoiding elaborations. If he aims to use the vocabulary familiar to the Junior Child (7–11 years) he will not be too far in advance of the infants and not too infantile for older children and adults. Assuming a pose of talking especially to the children usually becomes condescending and more confusing than if normal, clear language is used.

(*b*) *The children may be grouped together or scattered about the congregation.* Children will feel much more part of the congregation if they can sit with their parents or adult friends. The grouped Sunday School may be convenient, but it savours too much of a captive audience with guards (teachers) paraded for worship as a distinct body. Few children will thank the preacher who singles them out for special mention. 'Remembering the children' means remembering them as part of the whole congregation and we shall help them most by what we do for them by planning and conducting the whole service (or the part for which they are present) in such a way that they can share in it.

(*c*) *The preacher is remote from the children, and in many cases unknown to them.* The preacher should, therefore, not attempt to be 'pally' with the children or try to force a response from them. Children will accept him for his function and be quite happy if he carries out his role clearly. Questioning is always dangerous when the situation is unknown since children are reluctant to answer to a stranger. There is something to be said against pulpits, even in general worship, but a preacher does need to be seen and heard, and if to become more involved with the congregation the preacher leaves the pulpit he must be sure that he is still visible and audible.

(*d*) *The children are present for a short part of the service* and so experience only a fragment of Christian Worship. We should remember, though, that the shared part of the service does not end their worship. In class they will have the equivalent of lesson and sermon (the Ministry of the Word) and have a chance to make their response in a variety of ways which include prayer and giving. Because of this the preacher must not attempt to do too much. He should certainly not attempt an address since this is hindering the teacher who wishes to introduce the school theme. This part of the service will be dealt with in detail later. It is usually the opening of the service, but there is every good reason for the children to return for the offering and thanksgiving at the end of the service where they can join in the one action which unites us all, that of giving.

(*e*) *The Language of Worship* is in two forms:

(i) In hymns and psalms we express our feelings and

beliefs in image and metaphor. Combined with music these convey a sense of wonder and awe, joy and thanksgiving, or they can convey a more contemplative mood. Children can share in these sensations provided that the experiences they represent are real to the child. Hymns such as 'O worship the King . . .' or 'Immortal, invisible, . . .' may go far beyond the understanding of the child intellectually, but at the level of feeling they are real. Both represent, as well, God's greatness and goodness, concepts which are necessary to a child's religious development from an early age.

(ii) Poetic language in the spoken word, however, presents greater difficulties. Although there is great beauty in ancient prayers and versions of the Bible, archaic language will cause unnecessary confusion. With the revisions of our orders of worship we are discovering new beauty in contemporary phrasing.

In read prayers, lessons and our own extemporary language we need, above all, to be understood. It is too easy to allow ourselves fine sounding phrases which are puzzling to the children. They will take literally what we mean poetically. Preparation is therefore essential to prune and clarify our language. Impromptu praying is dangerous when children are present. We shall either forget the children and fall into phrases which are meaningless to the children, or attempt to simplify our language on the spot and end up with a kind of nursery prattle.

IV Children at Sunday morning worship

The situation which confronts most of us as preachers is that the children are present for the first part of the service and then go to their school. We can call this shared act of worship 'Our Approach to God':[1]

[1] This is 'The Preparation' of the orders of service on pp. 68–9.

> Remembering who God is—Adoration
> Remembering what we are—Confession
> Remembering God's forgiveness—Absolution
> The Dismissal.

The Sunday Service suggests that children stay in for the reading of the Lessons. This has the advantage that they hear the Bible read in the context of worship, but the difficulty has to be faced that much of the Bible is unintelligible to children, or likely to be misunderstood, and that it will add to the burden of teaching that the children have to sustain in the course of the morning session. There is no simple answer to this problem.

If the children do remain for the Lessons then it is imperative that we consider them. We can choose a lesson which will fit in with the Sunday School theme. Such a Lesson is published by the British Lessons Council. It will help to consult the Superintendent, and the more consultation there is the better. The new Lectionary has shorter lessons than those of previous ones and it is hoped that in future the B.L.C. Lessons will be related to it.

In reading the Lessons we should use a modern version and the complete *N.E.B.* now makes this possible. We should also introduce the lessons with *very* short (and prepared) introductions indicating the setting and the main feature of the passage. A teacher could be asked to read the Lesson. We must be careful, however, not to turn the reading of the Lesson into another teaching session. How far the theme of the whole service is to be determined by the presence of the children must be left to the preacher. It is better if he stresses the general elements of worship while they are present, making the theme explicit later.

How then can children be brought into this part of worship?

(*a*) *The Call to Worship.* This can vary from the informal:

'Good morning!' to a verse from a Psalm. Care should be taken that the Call to Worship does not simply duplicate the first hymn. In all cases it should clearly indicate that worship is beginning and what the congregation is expected to do.

(*b*) *The Hymn of Adoration.* The hymn of praise and affirmation comes naturally to children. They love making a 'joyful noise', and hymns which speak of the wonders of creation, the happiness of life, the love of God and his greatness, the life of Jesus come close to their experience. The general sections of the hymn book are more likely to provide the right material than that selected 'For Little Children'. Many (not all) of these are overworked, moralistic and tend to present an unfortunate brand of Victorian piety. In sharing in the great hymns of the Christian faith the children enter into a tradition which they will never outgrow.

It is important that the hymns are well known, singable and do not dwell on adult experiences which are foreign to the child. Community hymns are more suitable for both the opening of worship and for children than personal ones. The wide scope of hymns which children can use is evident in the *School Hymn Book of the Methodist Church* (M.Y.D.). The opening of worship is not the place for a children's hymn.

(*c*) *Prayer.* Children do not pray to order. Their personal prayers are spontaneous and unpremeditated, growing out of some experience in life which has moved them. Yet they can share in acts of prayer, especially if it is made clear what they are doing. The value of this will be more educational than devotional, but it will lay the foundations of a meaningful prayer-life later on. Prayer can be seen as valid if it is presented as something that they do. It is thinking, reflecting, remembering, being quiet and receptive. God speaks to us through our experiences, the needs of others, the world about us, other people, and awareness of these enables us to understand his will for us. Leading prayer is not only putting words into peoples' mouths or speaking for them, but suggesting thoughts which they can use, helping them to pray rather than praying for them. Prayer is joining in some communal activity, saying words or thinking about issues which bring us together and to God. If our aim is right we shall be able to use a variety of means of leading prayer with children present.

(i) We *do* something in prayer, and so it should be introduced as an activity: We *remember* God's goodness; ourselves, and what we are; we *think* about——; we *ask* ——; we *are quiet* so that——.

(ii) Guided prayer is helpful for children as it is for many adults. A thought can be suggested and then a short time for thinking about it.

(iii) Brevity is essential, as is the avoidance of eloquence.

(iv) Responses should be used wherever possible. The preacher should lead them in, having made clear what the response is before hand. Explanation about the prayer beforehand is never wasted, provided that it is simple.

(v) Communal prayers if rightly chosen are helpful to the child. To know some of the great prayers will give form and depth to personal prayer and unite him with other Christians. The General Thanksgiving, the Prayers of St Francis and Ignatius Loyola as well as the prayers in the official orders of the Church should become part of the vocabulary of the children of the Church.

(vi) Prayer grows out of experience of life, therefore the more we can call upon this the more real will prayer be. Ideally prayer should come at the end of worship when interest has been aroused and sympathy awakened, and this will be done in school. At the beginning of worship prayer is an act of preparation but it can still be expressed in terms of experiences of life.

(vii) Confession. The liturgical pattern demands that we confess our sins after we have praised God. This presents a problem where there are children and so it is important to know how to lead confession. But first a word about content rather than method. Confession is more than listing our faults, it is acknowledging what we are in the presence of the God who loves us and forgives us. It is because he loves us that we dare to confess, and we need to confess to be able to accept that love. Unless there is a strong conviction about the love of God children can be alienated from God by acts of confession. They know what naughtiness is and expect the consequences, but these are on the human level. Those who reprimand them are usually those who can be trusted and who show that they still love them. But if naughtiness is equated with sin, it becomes an offence against a God about whom they are anything but certain, so he is regarded with fear and mistrust. The harm that this does is seen in those forms of Christianity which harass guilt-ridden adults.

Therefore when children are present the love of God must be emphasized; that he loves us as we are, and that therefore we need not be afraid to be honest about ourselves when we think about him. In this we see how important an adequate declaration of forgiveness is, but neither confession nor forgiveness should be prolonged.

An example of the kind of prayer suitable follows:

> We have praised God for his goodness, now in the quietness of prayer we are going to think about him and ourselves.
> Let us pray:
> God is our Father and has given us all the good things we enjoy. (*pause*)
> For all your goodness:
> Response: We thank you Father.

Jesus has shown us how much God loves us, and so we can tell Him all about ourselves, the things that make us glad and our faults. (*pause*)

For all your goodness: etc.

He is glad to hear us and he forgives us. He is ready to help us by his Spirit to do what is right. (*pause*)

For all your goodness: etc.

In some cases it may be felt that it is more appropriate to delay the confession until the intercessions after the sermon when specific issues can be mentioned.

(*d*) *The Dismissal.* A hymn or psalm of praise is ideal for dismissal, but the children should not leave during it.

Some churches will ask for a prayer of dismissal. This should be very brief and not be in the form of a conclusion. The responsive form of *The Sunday Service* is most suitable:

Minister: The Lord be with you.
Children: And also with you.

V Youth and children's services

When children and young people are present for the whole service they must be taken into consideration, although we cannot altogether be limited by the comprehension of the youngest. In all cases:

The items of the service should be short and to the point;

As far as possible the theme should be of general interest to both adults and children, though at times within the service the interests of one group will predominate;

The purpose of each act of worship should be clearly indicated;

Preparation with all or part of the congregation should

be used to make the service a group activity rather than a solo performance;

There should be a clear pattern in the worship, for example, that followed in *The Sunday Service*.

VI Parade services

It is hoped that these will always be treated as Youth Services (see below). We should face the fact that in most parade services loyalty to the organization, rather than a desire to worship, motivates attendance, and in many cases there will have been adult pressure. The preacher must try to compensate for this by following the suggestions made above. He should not, however, single the young people out, but plan the service, choosing themes, lessons, hymns, and above all timing it with them in mind. Forty-five minutes should be maximum. The sermon can be designed to appeal to different sections of the congregation at different times, especially if there are young children present, but it should not exceed ten minutes. They should, of course, be actively involved wherever possible, and full use should be made of suitable visual aids. If the service is planned as a whole brief commentaries on each part of the service can lead up to the address and so help to reduce its length.

VII Family services

For these it is essential for the preacher to know the congregation or to share the service with someone who does. By its nature the service should be flexible so that the interruptions a family may cause are taken without embarrassment and woven into the service. In order to help create the relaxed atmosphere necessary a simple and familiar pattern should be followed. Items should be short, varied, and made very distinct. Participation is essential, so group preparation should take place, making it possible for others besides the preacher to share the leadership of the service and for the whole congregation to be involved. The theme, of course, must be of general interest, growing out of a common concern (e.g. families, holidays, why sing hymns, giving, etc.). A 'sermon' need not be a long talk; an idea can be developed by questioning, discussion, interviewing, making comments on a hymn or song, using visual aids, tapes or records.

Though we must consider the young people present in Parade and Family Services, themes should be significant enough to appeal to adults and there will be times when we cater for them specifically.

Anniversaries

If one is spared the traditional formalities which constrict anniversaries in certain parts of the country, these can be an excellent opportunity for the Sunday School to share its worship and concerns with the church. It is not a preaching occasion, and little good is done by 'getting at' children or parents (a strong temptation when we know this is the only time they attend church). It is the children's day and the preacher is there to enable the children (with the teachers) to lead worship. Nothing is so artificial as the traditional 'demonstration' with its trite moralism and dubious theology. Let the theme grow out of the normal work of the Sunday School. Meet the teachers well in advance so that the service can grow out of the current theme in the Lesson Notes. This will avoid meaningless rehearsal. Then present to the congregation the work done, each department talking about a particular section. This will avoid reciting, especially if the preacher can interview and question. Any talking he does will be in the way of introduction and commentary rather than an address.

There is no reason to neglect liturgical principles, in fact they will give structure to the theme.

The evening service of an anniversary can be taken either by the older departments, can concentrate on the teachers, or become a Youth Service.

Youth services

Adolescents have much to give, and want to give it, but they are insecure and uncertain of themselves. We find them shy or aggressive, apathetic or rebellious, and generally impatient with the adult world. They are unlikely to welcome the advice or exhortations adults think good for them. So, as in children's worship, we should think in terms of what we can help them to do rather than what we can tell them. They are naturally taken up with themselves and want to feel they matter. By asking them to share in making and leading worship we help them to discover their own potential and to work out their ideas in a concrete form. Teenagers are full of interests and have a serious concern about life but we have to listen to them and work with them to discover this.

Planning a Youth Service can be exciting and educational for both young people and preacher if it is carried out as a group enterprise;

(*a*) Meet well in advance and let the theme grow out of a free discussion based on their interests and needs, guided by the nature and purpose of worship.

(*b*) Explore fully the resources of the team, the congregation and the church building, thinking how these can be used and collecting material around the theme.

(*c*) Using a concordance or commentary, study the biblical aspects of the theme, deepening theological understanding and selecting readings for the service. This is where the preacher's training and thinking is essential.

(*d*) Think out how the congregation can be involved to save the service from becoming a performance.

(*e*) The theme should be developed in such a way that there is a point where it is made clear in an explicit form and its significance emphasized in some kind of sermon. This need not be long—nor in a traditional form, but without this the service loses its prophetic note.

(*f*) Prayer can be led in a variety of ways: a concern and silence, a song with time for reflection, reading together, using the newspaper, or with concerns put forward by the congregation or team members.

(*g*) The preacher will act as co-ordinator, editor (usually one is embarrassed by the wealth of material and selection must be ruthless) and director. His liturgical knowledge and awareness of the time factor will control what can become a shapeless string of items.

(*h*) It is important that young people should be made aware that in leading worship they are serving the whole church and working within a tradition which is larger than their own particular concerns and interests. They should, therefore, be encouraged to explore the meaning of worship and to consider the attitudes and needs of the older members of the congregation as they themselves hope to be considered.

VIII   Talking to children and young people

There are few occasions in public worship where a children's talk is suitable. The difficulties of communication are such that it is rarely effective and the work done in day and Sunday school render it unnecessary. In any case a preacher should not attempt to speak to children without knowing the recent research on children's religious understanding, otherwise he will do more harm than good.

If it is impossible to avoid speaking here are some guide lines:

(*a*) Be brief and attempt only one point.

(*b*) Avoid ready-made addresses and invented stories. Keep to reality.

(*c*) Choose topics within the range of children's experience.

(*d*) Avoid abstractions and use concrete instances. Children think literally and are easily misled by simile and metaphor.

(*e*) Analogy, a favourite form of children's address, is dangerous. What is comparison to us, may be taken literally by them.

(*f*) Biblical teaching is best left to the school where material suitable to the needs and understanding of the child can be selected. The danger of repetition is too great. Goldman found that 'too much' of the Bible was taught 'too often' and 'too soon', with the result that children rejected it.

(*g*) In telling a story one must grasp its significance and know its structure so well that the meaning can be made evident without elaboration, and that it can be told without reference to notes. Written preparation is essential.

In talking to teenagers it is essential to understand their attitudes, especially where religion is concerned. On the one hand they are insecure and therefore look to an authoritarian faith to which they can adhere, on the other hand they are critical and questioning about the tradition in which they have been brought up. It is within this tension that they are working out a personal faith for themselves that lies between dogmatism on one side and scepticism on the other. Both conviction and enquiry are essential if they are to continue to grow, for this is the stage when life is opening up for them, demanding new responsibilities and offering new freedoms. They are becoming aware of the world, of society, of themselves. They are working out their ideas and beliefs, falling in love, choosing their careers, facing the strains of examinations and generally adjusting themselves to the adult world. What they need above all at this time is the support which enables them to come to decisions openly with understanding and real conviction.

Too often at this stage preachers attempt to force young people into a commitment which is artificial and inhibiting, and young people respond to it because they are afraid to face reality. Commitment is necessary for young people but it must be in real situations and not through abstract theological theories. Their commitment is to learning about the Gospel and not to someone else's conclusions about it. Jesus asked his disciples for decisions only after a long probation of working and living with him. Adolescence is a time for exploration of the Gospel, and this is why the group method is so important. Commitment comes naturally as the faith becomes real, and the way to that faith is by fearless questioning. At this disturbing time of growth the real enemy is fear, and only a preacher whose faith is open and honest and so secure that he is not 'perplexed at being perplexed' can help them forward. Therefore in talking to them he will seek to talk *with* them, and explore rather than prove his point.

Useful Books

ON THE RELIGIOUS EXPERIENCE OF CHILDREN AND
YOUNG PEOPLE

Children in search of Meaning—Violet Madge (S.C.M. Press 1965)

Readiness for Religion—Ronald Goldman (Routledge 1965)

Teenage Religion—Harold Loukes (S.C.M. Press 1961)

Teaching the Christian Faith Today—Douglas Hubery (N.S.S.U. 1965)

Religious Education in a Secular Setting—J. W. D. Smith (S.C.M. Press 1969), chapters 8, 9 10

A Source Book of the Bible for Teachers—ed. Robert C. Walton (S.C.M. Press 1970), Part Two

Introductions to the Agreed Syllabuses: West Riding (1966); Wiltshire (1967); Lancashire (1968); Inner London (1968)

ON WORSHIP AND SOURCE MATERIAL

Worship for Today—ed. R. G. Jones (Epworth 1968)

Explorations into Worship—S. Hobden (Lutterworth 1970)

Words for Worship—ed. Campling and Davis (Arnold 1969)

Living—Liturgical Style RISK. Vol. 5, No. 1 (B.C.C. 1968)

Songs and other material from Bernard Braley, 191 Creighton Avenue, London N.2, especially: *Faith, Folk and . . .* series, ed. P. Smith

Useful material from C.E.M., Christian Aid and other charities

Specimen orders of service for when young people are present are being published by the Methodist Youth Department

7. Justification for Preaching

Brian A. Greet

PAUL'S logic in Romans 10:14–15 is faultless. Assuming the prophetic premiss 'Everyone who invokes the name of the Lord will be saved' (quoted in v. 13) he shows that invocation implies belief, and belief, hearing, and hearing, that someone has spoken. So the first necessity is for a preacher.

I The obligation to proclaim

The structured body of Christ—the Church—must have a voice. Its mere existence and activities are not sufficient in themselves. The 'Christian presence' must be expounded. 'Someone must interpret' (1 Cor. 14:27). When the members gather, it is reasonable to expect that the significance of their meeting will be explained and proclaimed. They are there not merely for mutual nourishment. Their existence testifies not only to the first part of Mark 3:14 ('that they might be with him'—RV), but also to the second part ('that he might send them forth to preach'— the commission which is amplified in the grand climax to Matthew's Gospel: 'Go forth therefore and make all nations my disciples'—Matt. 28:19 N.E.B.). Worship and mission are inseparable, and even if there be no unbeliever within earshot, no church service is complete unless the missionary obligation of the congregation is clearly articulated. This is the preacher's obligation. If the church door is the entrance for disciples ('learners'), it is also the exit for apostles ('those who are sent').

The gathered people of God are often confused. Their *raison d'être* is not always plain to them. They have come with a sense of need, and conscious that their presence implies willingness to undertake certain responsibilities. They need to be interpreted to themselves. This interpretation involves judgment (on their failure to fulfil their obligation to be Christ's body); encouragement (to strive more effectually and hopefully for this fulfilment); enlightenment (so that they see the truth more clearly); the promise of resources (to achieve the goal). The preacher is the agent of such interpretation. This is his obligation.

When a man recognizes and accepts these obligations, he stands in the 'apostolic succession', that is, the succession of those who know themselves to be 'sent' by Christ. 'As the Father sent me, so I send you' (John 20:21 *NEB*). The Lord's command is contemporary and inescapable. As Paul wrote: 'The love of Christ leaves us no choice. . . . We come therefore as Christ's ambassadors' (2 Corinthians 5:14, 20 *NEB*).

This is what we mean by a 'call to preach'. Jeremiah said, 'It is like a fire blazing in my heart' (20:9), or like the hot wind of the bare desert heights: 'In full blast it meets me' (4:11—G. A. Smith's translation in his Baird Lecture on Jeremiah, p. 69); while for Amos, all levels of the created world and the sum total of human history and experience bore witness to the vast sovereign purposes of God, whose most convincing demonstration of his power was the prophet's conviction that his own words rang out at the Almighty's behest. 'The Lord God has spoken. Who can but prophesy?' (3:8).

It is not sufficient for the preacher to have an academic interest in the forces that are shaking and shaping the Church today, and compelling contemporary man to re-examine his presuppositions about the nature of human existence. He must, like Amos, believe himself to be personally involved. He is aware that his environment has helped to fashion him and his ways of thought. But he also believes that he is helping to fashion his environment, to influence the beliefs and behaviour of his fellowmen. The preacher knows that such an assumption would be consummate impertinence, unless he believed that the compulsion to speak which grips him is the Spirit of God.

II Criticism of technique and authority of preaching

(a) Technique

Qualified people in the fields of education and modern techniques of communication need not look far to find a ready-made example of 'how-not-to-do-it'. Take a traditional church service at sermon time. A man, effectively cut off by being enclosed in a raised box, is delivering an oratorical monologue over a wide gulf of emptiness to an audience, passive, unresponsive and unquestioning, scattered at uneven intervals along straight and immovable pews. There are no visual aids, audience-participation, question time or expression work. Furthermore, the sermon could well be a set 'piece'; a model which the man made at home, and which he takes round to display at different centres where he is 'planned'. Indeed, it might even be part of a complete 'kit' (including 'suitable' hymns, lessons and prayers), the relevance of which to the situation of the people before whom it is unpacked and assembled is entirely fortuitous. The preacher is not always to blame. He may 'offer dates' to several circuits and be planned in many different churches over a wide area. He cannot be expected to know intimately each congregation. But he must be adaptable and ready to modify his material so that he speaks to the condition of his hearers.

In this situation a man must be relentless in his application to the study of the 'craft of the sermon'. The art is never mastered. Up to and including his last sermon, the preacher remains a learner. Yet he must never misconceive the nature of his quest for perfection. His aim is not to produce a homiletical masterpiece, but to fashion the finest possible tools for doing the work of an evangelist. Life is for living. It is not an endless search for 'quotable quotes' and 'illustrations'. A fanatical photographer might reach the point where he valued his family merely because they were useful models for his art. Let the preacher who reads, understand and take warning.

(b) *Authority*[1]

A pulpit utterance is not *ipso facto* authoritative. How then will the preacher's words come with authority to those who listen?

(i) For those who already accept the authority of Christ for their own lives, the preacher's words will come with compelling authority if it is plain to them that he is faithfully expounding what Christ was, did and said, and if the sermon becomes a 'means of grace' whereby Christ is effectually present to call, challenge, judge, forgive, heal, inspire, guide and commission. 'It is as if God were appealing to you through us' (2 Corinthians 5:20): nothing less than this awful responsibility, this ineffable privilege, provides the basis both of the subjective assurance and objective credentials of the 'herald of God' who, like his Lord, sounds 'the note of authority' (Matthew 7:29).

(ii) But how best to pitch this note: that is the preacher's

[1] See also chapter 8.

125

perpetual discipline. Contemporary man, in the classroom
or laboratory, on television, on the factory floor, or in the
pew, does not appreciate the categorical imperatives of the
Almighty 'roaring from Zion', thundering from Jerusalem
(Amos 1:2). Truth is not a series of propositions to be
accepted without question. The men of the Light Brigade
had not 'come of age': 'Theirs not to reason why'. But
people do reason why, and rightly. Only thus do they make
truth their own; only thus does it become part of experience. Truth is for doing (1 John 1:6, AV and RV).

It is virtually useless for a preacher to prepare a tidy,
orthodox discourse on 'eternal life', 'Salvation', 'the kingdom of heaven' or what have you, and deliver it as it
stands, unless his method of communication, language,
delivery, content, all combine to make the listener say to
himself, 'Why, that's *my* experience!'. Whilst it is the
preacher's task to widen and deepen the experience of his
listeners (or at any rate to show how that experience may
be widened and deepened), it is not his task to describe or
advocate something which is totally alien to their experience and which fails to touch their lives at any discernible
point. If a man is at point 'A', I do him no service by
describing how he may get from 'C' to 'D'. I have given
him nothing to latch on to. I must touch on 'A' (his
present experience) and clearly reveal the step to 'B' before
there will be any spark of response in him when I refer to
'C'.

(iii) However, a disembodied voice makes very little
impression. Where is this experience (described by the
preacher) exemplified? For those who do not accept
Christ's authority for their lives, the preacher's words will
be more likely to carry conviction if what he asserts about
Christ is seen to be assumed and embodied in the Church.

It follows that the preacher will need to meet objections
which must inevitably arise in the minds of the listeners

about the discrepancies between Christ's example and the Church's practice. This will involve a genuine attempt to grapple with specific ways in which the Church fails to measure up to Christ's stature. It will not do for the preacher to set up a few Aunt Sallies and knock them down again.

(iv) In all this, the preacher must be patently sincere, not only in his exposition of what he personally believes, but in his attempt to understand and answer the real objections of the unbelieving seeker after truth. The layman who is regularly working with people who freely criticize institutional Christianity and raise objections to the Christian interpretation of life can draw on authentic material to give the ring of truth to what he says.

It is not enough for him to state his own firmly-held convictions in a loud voice and leave it at that. He must also resist the temptation to give examples of the way in which he 'answered' his critics, or 'put them in their place'. He will not weaken, but rather will reinforce his statements if he can show that he has made them his own only after genuinely listening to the other man's viewpoint, carefully considering possible objections, and rigorously analysing opposing beliefs.

If we are not to discard the sermon what are some of the ways in which we can make it an effective instrument for communicating 'the sacred and imperishable message of eternal salvation' (Mark 16:8 *NEB*)?

III Possible answers

(a) Shorter Sermons

If a preacher is 'to serve the *present* age', he must come to terms with the way in which we are conditioned by our environment, and particularly by the mass media of communication. Most people *are not capable* of following a long and leisurely monologue in a hot (or cold) church, while they sit on hard pews, battling with the acoustics of a lofty building. At home they sit in comfortable chairs, can adjust the temperature of the room, sip coffee, control the volume of sound and see a man's face in close-up.

So the preacher must be extremely disciplined in his preparation. He must aim to say one thing; to say it briefly, clearly, convincingly and interestingly. The parables of Jesus are models of brevity. Who are we to try to improve on the Master?

A preacher with exceptional gifts may be able to 'hold' a congregation for twenty to twenty-five minutes while he goes through a carefully worked-out exposition of a Bible-passage or an important piece of Christian doctrine or apologetic. But it is far better for such a man to make the 'mistake' of opting for the brief, pungent, ruthlessly-pruned fifteen-minute sermon, than for the 'average' man to 'spread himself' and lose his congregation before he is two-thirds of the way through. Most of us are 'average'.

What we have said, however, assumes the 'traditional' sermon, that is, a homily prepared and delivered by one person. There are other forms in which the sermon can appear. Consider some of them.

(b) Dialogue preaching[2]

Two people prepare for this together. An older preacher ('A') might well share a dialogue with a younger man ('B'), to show how traditional and radical interpretations of the Faith may engage in fruitful encounter. 'A' might begin with a 'simple Gospel statement' like 'Christ died for our sins'. 'B' would immediately challenge him to put his faith into understandable modern terms. 'A's' reply would inevitably include more traditional language which would provide the occasion for further intervention by 'B' press-

[2] See chapter 4, pp. 71–3.

ing for clearer and simpler language. 'B's' 'come-back' could sometimes be destructive in the sense of wanting to eradicate antiquated and misleading words and phrases, but sometimes constructive in the sense of improving 'A's' attempted interpretation by saying, 'Could we put it this way . . .?'

Longwinded contributions to dialogue should be avoided. The aim is for each man to say his bit concisely and clearly, leaving it open-ended so that his partner can take up the argument naturally and pass it back to him in the same smooth and flowing way. This does not mean that there is never any 'conclusion'. Whilst the two participants must avoid an easily-contrived 'solution', they must be ready for the 'inspired' and prophetic word that may be given to either of them at any moment. There are times when no reply is called for. God reasons with his people thus far. They are prepared now for his authoritative and unanswerable command; his compelling and irresistible invitation.

Not only the sermon, but other parts of the service should be shared. 'A' and 'B' might share an antiphonal reading. The prayers might be divided so that 'A' leads prayers of adoration, confession and thanksgiving, while 'B' is responsible for the intercessions. If 'A' prefers the Authorized Version and traditional prayers, and 'B' the *New English Bible* and contemporary prayers, the whole service can help to illustrate and expound the need being expressed in the dialogue sermon.

(c) *Congregational participation*[3]

This is an extension of dialogue preaching. If the dialogue has been genuine, many members of the congregation will be eager to share in it. They will want to say 'Yes, but . . .', to ask questions and to make comments. It will

[3] See chapter 4, pp. 70–1.

greatly help the congregation in its participation if at least some of its members have been involved in preparation for the service. A preacher might be leader, say, of a group of teenagers which meets on Sunday mornings. His subject for the evening service could be discussed by the young people at their morning session, and some of them could accompany the preacher, ready to bring some of their already discovered insights to the congregation assembled for the evening service.

A preacher who has discussed his subject with the Men's Fellowship, Wesley Guild or Wives' Group, could ask some of the members to come to the Sunday service as 'a people prepared'. The presence and participation of a nucleus of people who do not have to take the service 'from cold' can bring immeasurable enrichment to the whole congregation.

(*d*) *Directed meditation*

This involves an appropriate use of silence. For example, the congregation can be given a passage of Scripture to read. The preacher gives them time to read it through, then reads it aloud himself and briefly expounds it. Then silence is given for the people to think about the exposition with the scripture open before them. They can be encouraged to discuss it with their neighbour in the pew, and put questions to the preacher arising out of their reading, study, thought and discussion.

(*e*) *Guided discussion*

A short sermon (8–10 minutes), delivered by one person, can prepare the way for group discussion among the congregation. A few carefully-worded questions, duplicated and distributed to the groups, can guide them to take up relevant points that have been made. The type of sermon envisaged here might well be a model for all sermons, though the length can be elastic. It is a monologue in form, but a dialogue in content; that is, it raises questions and gives answers which lead to further questions and so on, the material being arranged and presented in a way that invites enquiry. Again, this follows our Lord's method; he frequently asked questions (e.g. Mark 2:8-9, 19; 3:4, 24, 33).

Wherever a preacher decides to conduct worship along lines that will be unfamiliar to the congregation, or to introduce methods which call for their co-operation in ways which are strange to them, he must do all he can to take them into his confidence in advance.[4] New ideas suddenly 'sprung' on them without notice can confuse people, and even antagonize them to the point of vitiating all hope of the very co-operation which the preacher is seeking to encourage. 'Key' people, such as stewards and organist, should be put fully in the picture, and if circumstances preclude the possibility of informing the congregation in advance (some of them may not be present the previous week to receive the information), the preacher should patiently spend time at the beginning to explain the plan and purpose of the service and to ask for the people's sympathetic co-operation.

IV What can preaching hope to do today?

Preaching can put the Christian case. On radio and television inconclusive discussion and debate abounds. The mass media pour an unceasing stream of material into the public's ears. Trivialities are given space alongside events of momentous importance. A great deal of news is 'made'. We hear what the highly selective agencies give us. This is often inevitable. Reporters, cameras, microphones, etc., are not always where the truly significant things are

[4] See chapter 4, pp. 76-7.

happening. Even when all the equipment is in the right place, it is immensely difficult to give a 'true' picture. There is a vital place in contemporary society for the clear, straightforward statement of a case without everything being left 'open-ended', inconclusive and non-committal. Furthermore, the preacher does not depend on circumstantial evidence. It has its place, but he speaks of what he knows and testifies to what he has seen (cf. John 3:11).

Also, preaching makes explicit 'the missionary structure of the congregation'.[5] The 'comfortable pew' alluringly beckons Christians every Sunday. It seems to say, 'Come and slump here and be ministered to'. How hard it is to resist that temptation! Luther, indeed, described the Church as 'the inn and hospital of Christ'. But all customers and patients are on the staff. Worship is not a dose of tonic to buck me up to do God's work. Worship is part and parcel of God's total mission to mankind, in which I am involved.

The Christian congregation gathers only in order to be sent. 'Go forth into the world to live and work to God's praise and glory.' Preaching regularly reiterates the perpetual missionary obligation of God's gathered people, equips them to fulfil it, and maintains their enthusiasm for communicating the Faith with conviction, humility and intelligence.

Calls to worship, prayers and sermons provide ample 'cover' for many expressions which effectively obliterate the missionary dimension and add more cushions to the comfortable pew. No preacher ought to be without *The Prayer Manual* issued by the Methodist Missionary Society. Ask for it in the vestry. Courteously suggest it be commended to other preachers for regular use.

Beware of 'ghetto cliches', like invitations to the congregation to 'turn aside from the world', or thanking God for 'this opportunity to forget the cares of daily life', or

[5] See chapter 1, p. 29.

emphasizing 'this hour in the presence of Christ' in a way
that suggests all other hours are spent in his absence.

V   How can a preacher tell whether he is successful?

When the seventy returned flushed with excitement at the
'success' of their mission (Luke 10:17), Jesus told them to
rejoice not because the devils were subject to them, but
because their names were written in heaven. This enrol-
ment can hardly be paraded as proof of success; it carries
no present *kudos*. It is virtually impossible to measure
success in preaching. But a few negative and positive
pointers may help.

(a) *Negatively*

There are some reasonably clear indications that the
preacher is not being successful:

(i) when the congregation is obviously bored and in-
attentive;

(ii) if he never evokes criticism or opposition;

(iii) if people regularly tell him he has preached a good
sermon;

(iv) if he finds himself including material that draws
attention to his own achievements, or which tends to
depreciate other's gifts or to imply that other preachers
do not proclaim the genuine Gospel.

(b) *Positively*

Some intimations of success can be seen:

(i) when a member of the congregation takes up a point
of the sermon afterwards and wants to know more;

(ii) when a member of the congregation asks for specific
information about ways in which he can implement an
action which the sermon has challenged him to undertake;

(iii) when in conversation, or by letter, someone indicates particular ways in which a sermon has enlightened, helped, inspired or changed him;

(iv) when it later appears that, as a result of the sermon, someone made a commitment to Christ.

Yet the preacher knows that the fruit of success contains the seeds of destruction. The fruit grows on the tree 'in the midst' of the garden, good to eat, pleasing to the eye, tempting to contemplate. It is not to be eaten, for it feeds the pharisee in him, who thanks God that he is not as other men. Better leave the fruit intact and reach the day's end saying with the publican: 'Lord be merciful to me, a sinner'.

Useful Books

Dialogue with the World—J. G. Davies (S.C.M. Press 1967)
Worship and Mission—J. G. Davies (S.C.M. Press 1966)
Christ and Methodism—J. J. Vincent (Epworth 1965)
Ring of Truth—J. B. Phillips (Hodder & Stoughton 1967)
The True Wilderness—H. Williams (Penguin Books 1968)

8. The Authority of the Preacher

David Tripp

Who are you to stand up there and say that?

AN uncomfortable question, but not a surprising one: when a fallible man speaks before others of the profoundest issues of human destiny, of human nature's noblest possibilities and gravest ailments, we can hardly help wondering by what authority he does this. In our days, when all kinds of inherited beliefs are being questioned, and yet the mass media are trying to persuade us to believe all sorts of things, preachers must expect to have their authority questioned, and must also be prepared to guide those who are searching anxiously for a reliable authority. On top of any external pressures like these, if we know our own characters at all we cannot avoid asking ourselves: 'Who am *I* to stand up there and say that?'

Three different questions face us here: (1) What is the authority for the *institution* of preaching? (2) What is the authority of our *message*? and (3) What is our authority as *messengers*? We must remember that these questions are different: sometimes, people who are afraid of the Christian Faith think that they have escaped it because they can attack the lives of those who represent it; and sometimes we preachers, when we are afraid for our status as preachers, may be tempted to think that, because we can defend what we believe, we are ourselves beyond criticism.

The authority for the institution of preaching

Preaching is not a simple thing, but infinitely varied. Some of the prophets preached by signs, such as dramatic actions. The two preaching Orders of the Middle Ages had different policies for preaching: the Dominicans set out to preach 'by word and example equally', the Franciscans 'more by example than by word'. Even preaching in words can take many forms—our modern twenty-minute sermon, John Wesley's three-hour pleadings with the crowds, a provoking thought flung out in a five-minute broadcast. Whatever its outward form, however, all preaching has a common basis and a common authority.

Preaching is an activity that goes on between man and God. It is meant for man, for it brings news that he needs to hear. In a world of fear, bewilderment, self-disgust, rapid change, achievements of thought and skill, man needs some word of reassurance, reconciliation and purpose if his life is to be endurable. This fact is part of our authority to preach—but only if we have something to say. We *do* have something to say: that the living and true God comes to men with the offer of peace and life. To man in his need comes God in his mercy. This is our authority to warn the world and also to offer it the news of a divine love.

Christian preaching, then, is not advice or an exchange of views or an exercise in thinking, but good news of God. It is also news *from* God, for it is he who sends his messengers. He has entrusted the Christian Church with a commission to break the news to all creation (Mark 16:15—a verse from the second century, reflecting a hundred years or so of the experience of preaching and of Christ's presence with his preachers). Within the Church, preachers are given a personal commission for the same purpose, to be what the New Testament variously calls messengers, heralds, ambassadors or bringers-of-good-news. Selected, trained and commissioned by the Church, and then sent to our allotted places, we go with the authority of God. This is based on the inner nature of God himself; the Father sends the Son, and so the Son sends us (John 20:21), and so that this may be effective, the Holy Spirit is sent.

We need to have as full a knowledge of our message as we can, just as a lawyer must know his legal sources for his arguments, the statutes and cases that bear on the problem on hand. Yet over and above knowledge of this kind, and the authority which knowledge confers, we need a deeper kind of authority—that type of authority shown by Christ himself. He spoke as 'one who had authority', and not as a retailer of collected scholastic opinions (Mark 1:22). In the humility of his earthly life, this authority is not shown by the uttering of his own thoughts or the execution of his own plans, but in his speaking and acting as his Father wills. So we are told again and again in the Fourth Gospel (see John 5:19, 5:30, 6:38, 7:16, 8:42, 8:54, 14:10). Our true authority, like our Master's, is to be *under* authority.

We are subject to the authority of the Word. Our preaching work is often called 'the Ministry of the Word'. This does not mean only a service in which *words* are used. The Word is Christ himself; for in him the Father has approached us with mercy, and since he remains present with us in his Spirit he continues to be the standing offer of a new and deathless life. Our authority as preachers is our responsibility to Christ to make him known.

From the idea of preaching that we have just given, two main questions arise: Where do we find the authority of Christ that is to govern what we say? and then, by what authority may we, being the kind of people that we are, exercise this office?

The authority that is to govern our message

We find the authority of Christ in the Bible. To obey this source rightly, however, we need to appreciate its true nature. We know we cannot use the Bible as if it were a telephone directory, in which every line is as important as the next. We also know that modern research has made many people unsure which parts of the Bible can be relied on. A detailed account of the authority of Scripture must be left to our biblical and doctrinal studies; but there are three aspects of this book that we must mention here, for they show how the Bible governs our preaching.

Firstly, *the Bible is full of preaching.* The oldest books of the Old Testament as we now have it, the eighth-century prophets, are collections of sermons. Even the books of the Law are built around a preaching of what God has done to create his people—look, for instance, at Exodus 20–24. All the books of the New Testament, except Philemon and 3 John and possibly Acts, were written to be read aloud in the Christian congregations, almost as sermons. The letters of Paul are indeed sermons, very elaborate ones, to be delivered when the Apostle himself cannot be present to preach. Acts is full of examples of early Christian preaching. When we look at these facts, we ought to see that we are, as preachers, carrying on a chain of tradition that stretches through the ages from biblical times onwards.

Secondly, *the Bible itself preaches.* The way in which its events and thoughts were recorded and have been preserved shows that it is itself a testimony to, and a declaration of, God's mercy. This must surely be part of what we mean when we say that the Bible is inspired, however much more we may mean by that. We become colleagues of the Bible writers, as it were; just as they did, so now we are to testify to God's gracious dealings with his world. When we use the authority of the Bible in preaching, we cannot simply point to the pages of the Bible and shout: 'The Bible says . . .', and then assume that this answers every possible question or doubt. Rather, we have to learn to see the truth of God as the Bible writers saw it, and then commend it to the people of our day as faithfully as they did to the men of theirs.

Thirdly, we must know *the dominant theme of the Bible— God's revelation of himself to man's experience in growing measure through the years*. The process begins with one nation formed in years of wandering and rescued from slavery, and culminates in the coming of the Son to die for mankind, to rise in victory over evil, and to dwell in his Spirit within a Church Universal that would preach him throughout the world. This thread of thought runs through the Bible, holding it together—all the rest is commentary— and this is to be the central theme of our preaching too.

Then *we find the authority of Christ in the Church*—and, whatever some people may say, the Church and the Bible are not really opposed to each other. After all, it is the Christian Church that has preserved the Scriptures, and has decided which writings showed themselves by their character to be worthy of inclusion in the Canon, or authoritative list, of these Scriptures. The lasting existence of the Bible in the world has not been as a bundle of pages on a shelf, but as a living word glowing in the minds of Christian people. It is against such a background that the Church has, at various moments of temptation and decision, stated our belief on certain crucial matters in a solemn and deliberate manner, to protect Christians from errors that would undermine their whole faith. These deliberate statements, or 'dogmas' (*dogma* is Greek for 'decree', 'formal declaration'), we find in the Creeds and in such utterances as the Definition of Chalcedon, which receive attention in our doctrinal studies. They may seem unexciting, but they fulfil two very important functions.

Firstly, *they single out the principal features of the Bible record of God's self-revelation*. This is vitally necessary, for it is fatally easy for any of us to get so wrapped up in our pet theories and favourite themes as to neglect essential topics of our message. We need to be reminded which Christian beliefs are most important—this is what is called 'the proportion of the Faith'.

Secondly, *these statements clear up a number of disputed points on which the real value of the Christian Faith depends*. For example: the Church has decided that its preachers must portray Christ as being both truly human (or his coming would have been just an empty gesture, not an act of love), and also as being truly divine, 'consubstantial with the Father' (or his work for us could not be the divine deliverance of the world, and we could not worship him as Lord and God). Points like this have been clarified, not just for the sake of leisurely academic precision nor out of a bureaucratic lust for uniformity, but to guard the good news entrusted to us and to protect both us preachers and our hearers from error and blasphemy.

We further find the authority of Christ in the principles of that part of the Church to which we belong and are answerable. It is not nowadays popular to mention this, for we all know what evils can come from denominational pride. However, when all is said and done, we who preach under the aegis of the Methodist Church have a clear duty to be loyal to the tradition in which we stand: after all, we must be grateful for Methodism leading us to the knowledge of Christ; and if we cannot honestly represent its position we have no right to appear as its spokesmen. Yet there is more than loyalty at stake here, for 'our doctrines' have been formulated for reasons that give them a more objective authority. Leaving the details for our doctrinal studies, let us mention here just a few points about the position of

Methodism as we find it in the *Deed of Union* and in our official standards.

Methodism is committed to the Scriptures and the Creeds, and thus owes loyalty to the Holy Catholic Church, of which it is a part. Our Church is also committed to Protestant principles (for example, justification by faith, the authority of Scripture); and since there is disagreement among Protestants, Methodism has taken up a position on a number of controversial points. We teach that God's love is offered to *all* men, that priesthood as the New Testament understands it is exercised through the *whole* Church, that Baptism and Communion are divinely instituted and obligatory, that we may be assured of God's merciful favour, that God can and will perfect us in love by the power of his Spirit. For our study of authority, three observations about the Methodist *use* of doctrine must be made. One: we maintain that Christian beliefs are to be *preached* (that is why our doctrinal standards, Wesley's *Sermons* and *Notes*, are designed to set up standards of preaching), and so preached as to show God's power transforming human life, both in the individual and in society. Two: we are convinced that the preaching of the Gospel must be a team effort. The authority of our denomination lies in its being a *fellowship* in which Christ reveals himself through our common life. Hence the Circuit Plan, the Preachers' Meeting and the Lectionary, designed to guide our use of the Bible so that all the great points of our belief are regularly held up before our people, partly through the changing seasons of the Christian Year. Three: As both the *Sermons* and the *Notes* testify, we are open to correction on disputed points by other Christians of orthodox belief.

Lastly, *we find the authority of Christ in the experience of Christian people*. In a sense, of course, all that experience and reason tell of truth is an addition to our knowledge of

God, but not all such knowledge establishes a personal relationship with him. The experience of Christian people, in whom and among whom the Holy Spirit dwells, reflects the work of the Spirit as he leads us into all truth. We know how difficult it is to judge the value of experience; and for the purposes of the preacher Christian experience must be carefully tested against the standard of Jesus' coming to us (look at 1 John 4:1–3). However, the fruits of experience and reflection, both our own and other people's, show us the needs of men that most call for God's help, and so indicate the questions that preachers ought to tackle as matters of priority. The experience of the great saints also gives us some idea of the great power of the Holy Spirit. Even such experience cannot add to the substance of the Faith (nor take anything from it); but it can give most convincing illustrations of it.

The authority that entitles us to act as messengers

The message is there, and the need of it is there, but who are you and I to become the bearers of it? For we are fallible men, and sinners like everyone else. For all that, we are heralds of God.

Our authority for being so is that we have been called and appointed. We have been called inwardly, perhaps in a growing conviction slowly taking shape in quiet hours of thought, perhaps when someone has challenged us as to how we are going to serve God; for a very few, there may be an awesome moment such as Isaiah or Paul knew. The inward call is examined and tested and ratified by the outward call of the Church. Then we are appointed to exercise this calling. Even a Note to Preach is an authority, not only a formality; it gives the power to take some part in the work of preaching, so that our calling may be put to the proof. This calling and appointment put us in a position between the message entrusted to us and those to whom the message is to be delivered. In this position, our authority as preachers should mean both that we know what we are doing, and also that we understand the people that we are dealing with.

We are to speak as those who know what they have to say. We have authoritative sources for our preaching, and we must know them thoroughly. If our message is to come from these sources and to our hearers in an authentic form, then we shall have to speak, not merely as those who *have studied* our sources, but as those who *are studying* them still. On the other hand, our authoritative sources and our studies of them are not themselves the Word that we have to pass on. If our hearers, when we have finished, know the text of the Bible or the words of the Creed a little better, that is all to the good—but we are aiming at more than that. Our concern is that each one who hears us should, sooner or later, know that God is speaking to him. As Dean Goulburn wrote more than a century ago: 'Preaching is the appointed ordinance for turning the Word of God into the Voice of God.'

If that is to happen, we must know what people are, and know our own congregations personally, if we can. If we do not know how people's minds work, our preaching will almost certainly pass our hearers by. Paul's sermon on the Areopagus in Athens, which was not such a failure as some people think, is an example of a preacher weighing up his hearers, catching and holding their attention and so leading their minds to Christ. In the end, they have to make up their minds about Christ, some by rejecting him in scorn, some by putting the question off with an easy politeness, others by embracing the Faith.

Sometimes, like Paul, we may have opportunities to set forth our Christian beliefs to unbelievers. However, we usually have to do this more in personal conversation over months and years than in any formal discourse. None the less, even our sermons within the fellowship of the Church can help to commend the Faith to the world at large. As our people face the difficulties, objections and sometimes derision of their unbelieving neighbours, they need an inner conviction of the authority of God's Word, a Faith that they can grasp and stand up for. They should be able to expect our sermons to help them to get their bearings in Christian belief and practice, and to find encouragement in the very tone of what we say.

Most of the time we are preaching within the Church, and we have to remember this. The Church as a whole shares our authority for the service of the Word. By arranging for the preaching and then listening to it, the Church plays its part in getting the Gospel proclaimed, and offers the preaching to God as part of its regular worship. Since the whole congregation thus shares our responsibility, there is good reason for consulting them about our preaching and the conduct of services generally. We cannot neglect our final responsibility for all that happens in our worship, but consultation with Stewards, Leaders, specially constituted worship committees where they can be formed, or even with whole congregations, is to be encouraged.

One situation in which we obviously *must* have the two-fold authority of knowing both the Faith and also our hearers' requirements is when we have to preach on a controversial issue. Controversy is a dangerous activity that only a fool would rush into, but it is sometimes unavoidable. It is permissible only when the beliefs or moral standards of our congregations are being severely tested by anti-Christian propaganda. Then our people need controversial preaching; but they need it less in the form of the denunciation of error, far more in the form of the positive and attractive delineation of truth, a strong emphasis on Christ. The very nature of the truth as we have it in Jesus dictates the way we ought to conduct ourselves in the course of controversy. Since our Gospel speaks of God's self-emptying love, our attitude in controversy must be humble, and guided by love both for truth and for those whose views we must oppose. In everything we say in controversy, it is most important to show exactly what degree of authority is claimed for each point we make. Some things must be said *in Christ's name*, with an appeal to his full authority; while some things, however important, may be said *for Christ's sake*, but not as if we knew his will in detail. For example: we must say in Christ's name that justice (e.g. racial harmony) is a duty of mankind, and all injustice utterly wrong; but there is no one scheme of (e.g.) racial integration that can claim to have his authority—we can only beg our hearers for his sake to think carefully about the various plans that are put forward.

However well we know our Faith, however well we understand the needs of human nature, we still have to ask what authority we as individuals have to exercise such an office as this.

Our personal authority for the task begins with the inner compulsion to make Christ known: '. . . necessity is laid upon me. Woe to me if I do not preach the Gospel!' (1 Cor. 9:16, RSV). There is some further authority in our personal experience. The events that have moulded our life and the thoughts thrown up in meditation on great themes of belief and principle all go to make us a little more serviceable in the service of God. The authority conferred upon us by such experience seems to be threefold. Firstly, as our experience has done for us, it can perhaps help others to feel *the living reality of the Gospel*, and so interpret it. No experience of ours could of itself add to, detract from, or alter our essential message, but it may, if modestly and sparingly used, bring home the challenging presence of

God. Secondly, it can show a little of *the width and profundity of the Gospel*—not because we know all about it, but because we are learning how little we know about it, and how much we see that remains for us to know. If we, as honest people, acknowledge the limitations of our own experience in Christian living and thinking, some of our hearers may learn that they do *not* know all there is to know about the Faith—and some folk have an urgent need of that lesson. Thirdly, the limits imposed on us by our experience will to some extent dictate those *aspects* of the Faith we ought most to preach on, and the *approach* we ought to make to them. An act of worship as a whole should, in one way or another, assert all the chief points of our belief, but a sermon has to be selective. Apart from the limited time, there is another limit set by our degree of spiritual maturity. Some Christian doctrines must wait for us to preach on them until we have in our turn come to see their importance, for preaching is only really convincing when our whole personality stands behind what we say. ·

There is a sort of authority in our own unworthiness—in two senses. On one side, that God should use for the declaration of his love such quite unworthy persons as we are, is itself a mark of the depth of his mercy. When our hearers appreciate this, they will be able to see beyond us to the God who deigns to employ us—and we find that the authority of the Christian preacher makes him transparent. On the other side, our unfittingness for this task shows us that all the types of authority we have just thought of are no help at all without the living power of the Holy Spirit, the Comforter, the inspirer of all true sources of authority, by whose cleansing presence alone the sources will show the truth and our personalities reflect it. In the words of Calvin: 'God's Word is uttered by men like ourselves; common men who may even be much inferior to us in dignity and social importance. But when some insignificant little man is raised up out of the dust to speak God's Word, he is God's own minister'—but only when we are open to the Spirit, praying for his help: 'Almighty God, cleanse my heart and my lips that I may worthily proclaim your Gospel.'

Useful Books

ON AUTHORITY IN GENERAL

Vision and Authority—John Oman (Hodder and Stoughton revised ed. 1928)

ON THE BIBLE

The Authority of the Bible—C. H. Dodd (Nisbet 1928; Fontana 1960)

Is the Bible Inspired?—John Buraby (S.P.C.K. 1959)

ON PREACHING

Lectures on Preaching—Phillips Brooks (1877, recently reissued by S.P.C.K.)

Positive Preaching and Modern Mind—P. T. Forsyth (Hodder and Stoughton. 2nd ed. 1909)

The Apostolic Preaching and its Development—C. H. Dodd (Hodder and Stoughton 1936)

The Servant of the Word—H. H. Farmer (Nisbet 1941)

A Faith to Proclaim—J. S. Stewart (Hodder and Stoughton 1953)

The Ministry of the Word[1]—R. E. C. Browne (S.C.M. Press 1958)

Paul on Preaching[1]—J. Murphy-O'Connor (Sheed & Ward 1964)

What's Wrong with the Church?—H. Thielicke (Hodder and Stoughton English ed. 1966)

The ABC of Preaching—D. Francis (Epworth 1968)

[1] Rather more advanced.

In Church

Preaching Today—D. W. Cleverley Ford (Epworth/S.P.C.K. 1969)

About Preaching—Ed. John Stacey (Local Preachers' Department, Methodist Church 1970)

9. Sources of Sermons

Wallace H. White

A PERSON is not qualified to preach unless he is firmly committed to Christ, conscious in his own life of the love and goodness of God and in possession of a steady conviction that he is called to offer the Gospel to others. As this experience of God develops with the years it will not only inform his preaching but will drive the preacher on to seek new and more effective ways of equipping himself for his calling. If however he preaches only from his own experience, his sermons will be very limited and he will be unable both to minister to the differing needs of his various congregations and to expound the full range of the Gospel. Unless he grows he will soon become a bore.

So this chapter deals with that hard grind of long term and short term preparation for preaching, a discipline which the totally committed person cannot escape and indeed will not want to escape. He will be unable to offer anything but his best to God and his people and will be driven on to disciplined study and the acceptance of sometimes uncongenial and irksome preparation. Without it the sources of sermons will never be equal to the demand. What Maxim Gorki said about the writer is true of the preacher: 'There must always be a hedgehog under his skull preventing his being at rest.'

Everyday life

It cannot be emphasized too strongly that the major source
of sermons for a local preacher is his secular life. Some
preachers are tempted to opt out of the turmoil of full
participation in contemporary life, to touch secular life as
little as possible, to surround themselves—in reading,
friendships, interests—with the Christian and the devout.

This is to be untrue to the calling of lay preacher. Such
people have a specialist vocation as worker priests. They
are called to live in the world and to speak of the Gospel
to men in the same situation. They know from individual
experience the strains and temptations and pleasures of
living in the secular. They can understand the ways of
thinking and the problems of their fellow laymen and the
things that weigh most with them, in a way which those
outside the situation find very difficult. What others may
call 'labour relations', 'differentials' and 'productivity
agreements', such people know on the personal, practical
level. If they are to be preachers to today's congregations
they must be people of today. If they are, they have an
unrivalled source of sermons that speak to their contemporaries' real needs. They will be able to preach in the
language people use—not theological jargon or the outmoded vocabulary of a previous generation.

Contemporary sources

Contemporary sources of sermon material of the highest
importance are the newspaper, television and radio programmes, the theatre and the cinema. Here are pictures of
the world as it is and a knowledge of human nature far
broader than a person's individual experience. Politics,
psychology and the wonders of modern science highlight
the world for which Christ died and to which preachers are

called to proclaim the love of God. Articles and discussions by agnostics and humanists stretch the preacher's mind and open up the objections to faith that his hearers have to face. Journals such as *The Listener*, the *New Statesman*, *The Spectator* and *The Christian Century* often contain such stimulating material and are to be found in the reading rooms of local libraries. Regular study of a good daily newspaper is also essential.

Books

So being a man of his own day, the preacher must be aware of the danger in some excellent classics often recommended to him. A preacher should be well read with a stored mind to draw upon but some of the classics of the spiritual life and biographies of outstanding Christians can be a snare unless it is remembered that they come from a different world from that of the second half of the twentieth century. *Of The Imitation of Christ* and *The Pilgrim's Progress* have an undisputed value; but they have to be seen in their historical and psychological context before their lasting contribution can become part of the preacher's own faith, finally to enter his sermons. Such classics must be balanced by modern authors who are writing for today's situation. Valuable insights can be gained not only from religious books, but from secular writing and from modern novelists, and the bibliography at the end of this chapter contains a number of suggestions of this kind.

Unless the preacher has a phenomenal memory which he can be sure will last into old age, much of this valuable background will be lost without a way of anchoring it and keeping it available. Some keep a book of cuttings. Some have a card index of subjects referred to in the books they have read. Others make notes at the back of their books.

Each preacher has to work out the method he finds most helpful. But the unmethodical add to their troubles and their congregations find that their sermons lack a certain richness they might have had.

Books of sermons

Books of sermons may be mentioned mainly to be discouraged. The great classical preachers spoke under different conditions and to different people from us (and at greater length!). Their work is of value mainly as a picture of men of another generation trying to make the Gospel real to their contemporaries. A few books of sermons are still published and can be of help in showing us masters of the craft applying the Gospel to today's need. But beware imitating their style. What is natural for one man can be downright absurd in another. And overcome the temptation to filch their illustrations. Others have inevitably been there before you and you will be reproducing the hackneyed, to your congregation's boredom or amusement. In periods of mental dryness, when no ideas will come, such books can perhaps help to prime the pump. But beware the temptations!

The Bible

The preacher should preach out of a full mind. He should be well informed, using modern mass media, as well as the broadening and deepening powers of biography, history, drama, poetry and the great novels, in addition to the technical studies of his own specialized calling. If he cultivates an alert mind he will be spared the incessant search for sermons, and will find ideas coming unasked as he watches a television programme or walks down the road on a spring morning or sympathizes with an anxious friend.

But he will always turn to his Bible.[1] Here the Gospel is to be found in preparation or fulfilment. Here are men and women in all their complex relationships with God and each other. Here the love of God blazes out in Jesus Christ with a light that illumines all other experience. We can never overestimate the value of this book to the preacher. It is his sourcebook *par excellence*.

The Methodist Lectionary[2] contains five lessons for each Sunday (Morning: Old Testament, Epistle and Gospel; Evening: Old Testament and New Testament) and it is no bad discipline to read these, one each day prior to the Sunday to which they apply. Such reading can often produce sermons.

The Bible is a dangerous book. People bring to it their preconceptions and can find in it what they wish. The freedom fighter of Zambia or the Dutch Reformed apartheid supporter of South Africa appeals to the same book. It has been used to prove that the sun revolves round the earth and that witches should be burnt.

It is also a very difficult book. At the end of his letter, the author of II Peter talks of the wisdom Paul uses in his writings, 'though', he says, 'they contain some obscure passages'. Our sympathy is all with the author of II Peter! Books by other writers, too, need a specialized knowledge to understand their meaning fully; the letter to the Hebrews can be appreciated only by a reader with a working knowledge of Jewish sacrificial theology and practice and the Book of Revelation by one who understands the principles behind first-century apocalyptic literature. Even some sayings of Jesus are by no means self-evident, e.g. 'All who came before me were thieves and robbers'; 'The man who has will always be given more; but the man who has not will forfeit even what he has'; 'If anyone comes to me and

[1] See chapter 8, pp. 138–140.
[2] See chapter 5, p. 86.

does not hate his father and mother, wife and children, he cannot be a disciple of mine'.

So preachers have to be not just Bible readers but Bible students. They must master the meaning of this book. They must delve below the surface for the precise significance and the accurate interpretation. Not for them a few verses read sleepily before bed or a mere familiarity with the beauty spots. They have to wrestle with the text until the exact meaning is theirs. Then—an even more difficult task—they have to interpret the meaning for their own people, tearing it out of the outmoded thoughtforms of two thousand years ago and reclothing it in language significant for their hearers and applicable to their specific needs.

This is work that might daunt the most able and preachers need to use the very best help that is published. And very much is. Commentaries abound. Not just the popular lightweight books—these are not for the Bible student— but the more detailed scholarly series, one volume to each Bible book. With the guidance of a more experienced preacher, the novice can build a library of commentaries, buying the best volumes from each series. To them can be added such background books as a complete concordance, a Bible atlas, studies of the parables of Jesus and of his other sayings and a good theological wordbook of the New Testament.

The preacher will make sure, also, that he possesses as many Bible translations as he can afford.[3] Comparing them will often shed new light in unexpected places in his preparation and help to make the scripture readings, when he is conducting worship, more intelligible to his hearers. Such books as these will help him to discover the timeless meaning of the Biblical passages so that he can retranslate

[3] See chapter 5, p. 89.

them for his own hearers and open out for them the contemporary significance of the eternal Gospel.

Sometimes in his studies a text will take hold of the preacher's mind so that he has no alternative but to preach from it. He should then make certain that he knows what was its exact meaning in Biblical times and what is its meaning and message for his congregation today. If he is using a Bible verse in this way, the preacher must be quite sure that he does not twist its meaning, drop it half way through the sermon or merely use it as a peg for other ideas.

From time to time a longer passage from a Biblical book calls for exposition. So long, once more, as the preacher does his homework, using his commentaries to discover the exact meaning, this can be very valuable for a congregation. So, too, can be the exposition of complete books of the Bible. The little book of Ruth has a real message in this day of racial prejudice. Paul's letter to Philemon illustrates the revolution that the application of the Christian faith to personal and social issues can have.

But a sermon is not improved by interlarding it with scripture quotations. However effective this may—or may not—have been in days gone by, modern congregations find the piling up of scripture quotations tends to bore rather than enlighten or convince. Let the preacher be enough a man of God to stand on his own feet and preach what he trusts is God's truth, without propping up his self-confidence and his message by such means.

Text or subject?

Many preachers today do not start with a text at all. This, of course, is not a modern gimmick but was the practice of the Church for the first twelve hundred years of its life.

It is argued sometimes that the Bible is the Word of

God, the textbook of our faith, the basis of our religion; and to start from a Biblical idea means that the preacher is more likely to continue with Biblical truth. It is only too easy to import one's own prejudices into sermons—quite unconsciously—and a text-based start can help to prevent this. However bad the sermon, the congregation can take away at least one nugget of God's truth.

In practice, these arguments are of only limited validity. Many an heretical sermon has started from a text—and so has one full of prejudice and ignorance of Christian truth. Indeed, many listeners know so little either of the Bible text or of the Bible world, so different from that of the twentieth century, that a preacher who starts with a text may have to spend too large a proportion of his sermon time on background explanation before he can elucidate the meaning for a congregation of today.

For many, such an approach seems artificial. A preacher should stand up as a man or woman of today's world talking to his contemporaries about the Christian faith, its meaning, problems, application and attractiveness. One of the primary lessons a preacher must learn is that he has to start where his people are if he is to lead them to where he wants them to be.[4] It was once said that if you are playing dominoes and your opponent puts down a double six, you have to start with a six yourself. So with preaching. We are not talking to 'Man' but to certain specific people with quite definite needs and problems, living in a known environment. The preacher has to start from life as his congregation knows it. So he can preach on a subject much in the news; a natural calamity; a local election; the latest criticism of Christianity on a television programme. Some contemporary problem or public happening already in the congregation's mind is an admirable opportunity to explain what Christianity has to say and to lead on to

[4] See chapter 7, p. 126.

perhaps wider and deeper issues. Or one may start with one of the major problems of living—the paradox of suffering; standards of sexual behaviour; the possibility of following Christ's way in business. These are perennial subjects but do not need a text for a preacher to expound what is the Christian approach to them.

In such preaching the preacher proceeds from the 'life-situation' to the Bible for the illumination and guidance he can find there.

Team preaching

Preachers today have an increasing opportunity to work together in the choice of their subjects and in preparation for their sermons. Many Circuits now undertake team preaching. Those who are to preach in, for example, Advent or Lent, meet together to plan sermon subjects for each Sunday. They can undertake their basic preparation together, meeting for reading, discussion, prayer and the sharing of experience and opinion. This may sometimes stretch the mind, especially of newer preachers, but the work on unfamiliar themes or subjects can be invaluable both for preachers and congregations. And the Holy Spirit can inspire this kind of sermon preparation just as satisfactorily as he can individuals studying in isolation.

The Christian Year

One of the major influences on a preacher is, of course, the Christian Year. Starting from Advent, with its theme of the Judgment of the world, he can lead his people in preparation for the coming of Christ at Christmas and his presentation to the whole world at Epiphany. Before Lent, he can concentrate on Christ's life and teaching and in Lent itself help his congregations to prepare, by self-discipline of mind and spirit, for the events of Passiontide, Palm Sunday and Holy Week. He can lead them through the triumph of Easter Day, the significance of the Ascension and the contemporary meaning of Whitsun to the celebration of Trinity Sunday. The following Sundays of the year give ample opportunity for emphasizing the outworking of our faith in daily living and of remembering such occasions as Church Anniversaries and Harvest Festivals.

In following this order, the preacher and his congregation are at one with the vast majority of the world church and this knowledge can bring a deep richness to the act of worship. As Raymond J. Billington pointed out in the previous book in this series, 'One small but valuable way of recognizing this link is by using the Collect for the Day at some point in the service. Not all of these (found in the full Book of Offices) are of equal merit, but many are models of succinctness, beauty of expression and devotional insight. Their use is a reminder of—and a bond with—many other Christians.'[5]

Most preachers have their own hobbyhorses, the themes they emphasize and those they forget. The Christian Year means that they cannot easily neglect some essential element of the Christian faith; and the extra work and application of mind and soul, for both preacher and congregation, wrestling with unfamiliar themes, is all to the good. The danger for Methodist congregations of having to listen to many different preachers is that they will not receive a balanced diet of worship and thought; but if the preachers follow the Christian Year this danger is largely negatived, congregations being reminded of the great themes of the faith and being given a definite pattern for their private devotional life.

[5] Morrow, Billington and Bates, *Worship and Preaching*, Epworth, 1967, p. 156. The Collects are now to be found in *Collects, Lessons and Psalms* (Methodist Publishing House)

At the same time they will be delivered from that endless round of 'special' occasions—which can so easily become just self-regarding and even trivial—and lifted up, to see and grasp the greatness of the Gospel.

Gordon Rupp's comment is apposite here:

'If we are going to treat the Christian Year seriously we should see that we have the whole coherent story of redemption pegged down in scripture, hymn and preaching. We shall not lightly set aside the joyful mystery of the Epiphany for Men's Sunday, the painful mystery of Passion Sunday for Young People's Day, the glorious mystery of the Ascension for Women's Weekend. It is as the Church lives closest to God's mighty acts that it becomes most adventurously human.'[6]

Types of sermons

With a Gospel as rich and varied as ours, the preacher has to learn to present all its facets to his congregations. There are some who, wherever they start, always end at the same favourite topic—to the secret amusement or annoyance of regular worshippers. New preachers often have to fight the temptation to call their congregations, on every occasion, to a decision to follow Christ—forgetting that usually the majority of their hearers are mature Christians needing guidance for Christian living or help up the steep places of life or the stimulus of a wider vision. As preachers have tried to speak to the varying needs of Christian people and present the Gospel in all its aspects, they have found it necessary to preach in different ways. Some of these ways can be classified as follows:[7]

Many sermons are explanatory. The preacher may find

[6] Quoted by Raymond J. Billington, op. cit., pp. 156–7.

[7] This classification is for the sake of clarity. Sermons are often combinations of these categories.

a parable of Jesus that is difficult to understand or a passage of Paul's that he feels has a message for his next congregation, so he sets about making the exact meaning as clear as he can, until the congregation not only see the meaning but feel its challenge or its strength. Or it may be that there is one aspect of Christian belief the preacher feels his congregation needs explained to them. Once again he studies it thoroughly until he himself is quite sure what it means. Then he makes it as clear and as attractive as he can for his congregation. The need to explain the Bible and the faith in this way is one of the major sources of sermons, which are then usually called expository.

But sometimes the preacher has to make out a case. He feels that circumstances have arisen that appear to invalidate the Christian claims. Perhaps there has been some natural disaster. Perhaps a well-known figure has been arguing against Christianity. So the preacher starts from rock bottom and builds up the Christian case, bit by bit, until he has shown that even if it is not subject to mathematical proof, at least the weightier probability is on the side of belief and not unbelief.

Many congregations show greatest interest in the practical implications of their faith. 'What does it mean to love God and our neighbour in this situation?' is their unspoken question. A local election will call for Christian leadership from the pulpit. The preacher must not hide behind pietistic generalities. The people want to know what a Christian should do, on what principles he should vote, and it is the preacher's plain duty to give real guidance on how they should make up their minds. Parliament may be debating aid for World Development. The subject is in the air and the congregation should be able to expect precise Christian thinking presented to them on the issue. Thus many of the ethical and social concerns of today give the preacher a clear lead on what he should speak about.

Many Christians find grave difficulties in their personal devotional life. Their need is a call to the preacher for help. Many of these problems can best be dealt with in dialogue sermons[8] or in smaller groups meeting in homes, where the informal and relaxed atmosphere helps frankness and honesty. But there are times when the preacher should talk in the pulpit of the problems and techniques of prayer; of the best ways for a layman to study his Bible; of new insights into the special problems modern man faces when he thinks about God.

There are times, too, when congregations need to be faced quite bluntly with making a choice—to be on Christ's side or not. In the past religion has often been presented in too individualistic a form; 'preaching for conversion' has been overdone or done in an ignorant fashion; but it is still true that there are occasions when people have to be asked what they really believe and to be challenged no longer to sit on the fence. Such preaching needs the lightest of touches or it can degenerate into spiritual blackmail or become embarrassing in its ineffective bad taste. But for the sake of spiritual health there are moments when men and women have to be faced with such basic questions.

Today, sermons do not always come in one piece. Except in church, people rarely listen to undiluted talking by one person for anything like twenty minutes. So preachers sometimes divide their sermons by a prayer or a hymn. We have learnt, too, that you cannot bludgeon the truth into people. Nobody likes to be told what to do. Too dogmatic an approach engenders a reaction; people become contra-suggestible. So our sermons need to persuade and convince, to make the truth look so attractive that it cannot be resisted. Indeed, sometimes sermons do not

[8] See chapter 4, pp. 71–3 and chapter 7, pp. 128–9.

answer questions at all but ask them, leaving the sermon to continue after the service in the minds of the congregation as they wrestle with the problem.

Making sermons

Finally, with all this preparation made, how does a preacher start writing his sermon? Material has been gathered from Bible study and life and experience. He has stored his mind with as wide a knowledge as possible. He knows at least a little of the need of congregations and of their reaction to preaching and of the kind of sermons appropriate to different situations. Now what?

Fortunately, if he has prepared in this fashion the preacher will never have to start from cold. Nor will he have, save rarely, the preacher's nightmare of a service on Sunday and not a thought in his head by Saturday night. More probably, he will have a mass of ideas and facts and possibilities. And there is not one right way to turn all this material into a sermon. Some people slowly construct a logical outline. Others see the sermon skeleton in a flash of insight. Some can only work at their best under pressure; others find that deciding on their subject well in advance leaves their subconscious to do much of the preparatory work for them (John Donne never went to bed on Sunday until he had the outline of the following Sunday's sermon on paper). But whatever method is best for the individual personality and temperament, there are some things everyone has to do:

1. Know where you are going. Define your aim. [9] Be humble enough to write it in cold ink on a sheet of paper and keep it in front of you. At the end, ask, 'Have I done what I meant to do?'

[9] See chapter 10, p. 165

2. Construct a logical sequence of thought[10]. Don't be afraid of scrapping what you have written and starting again—and again—and again.

3. Ruthlessly reject any material—however good—that is not relevant to *this* sermon.

4. Unless you are an exceptionally gifted person, write it out word for word. The discipline of doing this will be invaluable in unmasking diffuse expressions, clarifying thought and helping the memory.[11]

5. When the sermon is constructed, go through it all again and look for undigested technicalities. If a preacher is difficult to understand he is not usually profound but lazy.

This is part of every preacher's basic discipline in sermon making. Further and more detailed suggestions will be found in the next chapter.

Useful Books

Modern English Usage—Fowler (Oxford University Press, revised ed. 1965)

Roget's Thesaurus (Longmans, Penguin 1967)

Cruden's Complete Concordance (Ward, Lock & Co. and various eds.)

Atlas of the Bible—Grollenberg (Nelson 1959)

Everyday Life in New Testament Times—Bouquet (Batsford 1959)

A Theological Word Book of the Bible—Richardson (S.C.M. Press 1963)

Letters and Papers from Prison—Bonhoeffer (Fontana 1959)

God's Frozen People—Gibbs and Morton (Fontana 1964)

Come out the Wilderness—Kenrick (Fontana 1965)

[10] See chapter 10, pp. 166–8.
[11] See chapter 11, p. 180.

MODERN NOVELS

The New Man—Snow (Penguin 1970)
The L Shaped Room—Banks (Penguin 1969)
A Kind of Loving—Barstow (Penguin 1968)
The Chosen—Potok (Penguin 1970)

COMMENTARIES

No commentaries on books of the Bible are suggested since new ones are continually being published. The preacher should consult his minister or write for advice to the Local Preachers' Department.

10. Sermon Structure

Norman Graham

'His sermon had about as much structure as a bowl of porridge.' This somewhat unkind remark was heard after a Sunday morning service from a worshipper who was feeling cheated. What did he mean? He probably meant that for him what the preacher had to say didn't add up to anything, that nothing happened. If a problem was posed it wasn't answered. If answers were given the problem wasn't apparent. The sermon didn't seem to go anywhere. There may have been fervour, sincerity, interesting illustrations. There may have been a potentially arresting message, but in the absence of a clearly thought-out plan which carried the thoughts and feelings of the hearers forward in an orderly progression the end result was only confusion and dissatisfaction. The aim of this chapter is to consider structure in sermons as those qualities of order and sequence which enable it to 'connect' with the active processes of thought, perception, ideas and attitude formation which are continuously going on in the minds of people.

Few would object to the idea that persuasion is an important ingredient in the purpose of a preacher. He is concerned to change or modify attitudes and to help people to reorganize their mental life so that all which pertains to

Jesus Christ comes to exercise an ever increasing dominion over everything else in their lives. This purpose can be accomplished by supplying new and significant information. It can also be accomplished by convincing demonstrations in personal experience of the benefits of the Lordship of Christ. Again, humour, argument, the tracing of the consequences of refusal can all play their part. But all of these will be of no avail if the hearer cannot 'relate' to what the preacher is saying. It may be assumed that the hearer *is* actively trying to relate what the sermon is about to what he is, what he already knows, what he thinks and the problems he has. The preacher, by the way in which he organizes his material, as much as by the substance of it, can assist that process or he can frustrate it. He can assist it by ensuring a logical and clear progression in the different parts of his discourse. He can frustrate it by presenting his thoughts in a confused, unconnected, diffuse kind of way.

To test whether a sermon which is in course of preparation has form and structure it is absolutely necessary to reduce it to an outline. Such an outline should include a brief statement of the objective the preacher has in mind in delivering that sermon at all. Grand sounding, overarching objectives are of less value in guiding a discourse to its goal than more specific and limited aims. Thus all sermons will have as their objective 'To bring people to a knowledge of Jesus Christ', but a particular sermon will probably have a more specific and limited goal within the grand perspective. For example, to aim to 'teach them about forgiveness' is not as useful an objective as 'to show that the forgiveness the Christian exercises in his life is dependent on Christ's forgiveness'. The preacher must be able to give a clear statement of the more limited aims he hopes will be accomplished in this particular twenty minutes (or less).

After this should come a series of brief statements which sum up the content and main lines of argument. These will describe the steps by which he hopes to lead his hearers from where they stand initially to where he hopes they will stand at the end of the sermon. The number of steps or units to be used is a matter of personal choice. Traditionally three are recommended and by and large this is a good rule. There is no absolute reason why it should be three and not two, or four or more except that the number is probably better kept within the bounds of ordinary human memory. The more specific aim suggested above for a sermon on the theme 'forgiveness'[1] might be followed by setting out three lines of 'treatment', for example:

  (i) As applied to things which need not be forgiven.
 (ii) As applied to things which can be forgiven.
(iii) As applied to things which 'cannot be forgiven'.

Having sorted out from the material the main movements of thought, each one should then be broken down into its component parts and tested for logical sequence. The first section only need be considered here. Under the heading 'Things which need not be forgiven' might be listed such points as the following:

(a) Christians may be too ready to detect injury.

(b) Love is slow to anger—takes no heed to itself.

(c) It is therefore 'unseemly' for a Christian too readily to assume a sense of injury. Love, in this sense, is 'slow to forgive'.

(d) Forgiveness is unnecessary where no evil is perceived.

(e) Notice the 'style' and manner of Christ's attitude to injury. The same style should characterize the attitude of the Christian.

[1] The idea is derived from a book by Charles Williams entitled *The Forgiveness of Sins*.

The sequence of points should be stated as briefly as possible in this way. One should lead naturally and logically into the next. The sequence should form a coherent whole. If it does not the transitions may well prove awkward to make in delivery. This will interrupt the continuity of thought and so affect the concentration of the hearers. Each part sets up certain expectations about the general trend. If what comes next bears no discernible relation to those expectations then a certain sense of disappointment and bewilderment may be set up. If the preacher appears to drop a line of thought which was relevant and important to the hearers he may not be able to recover their attention and the sermon will fail of its purpose. The clutch has slipped. The gears of thought are no longer engaged.

The preacher now has a statement of his objective, a few main headings setting out the principal movements or sections and several subheadings each of which contains the specific or concrete content of the section. This outline is a ground plan and manifests the logical contours of the sermon which can now be envisaged in its entirety. It constitutes a mental map with signposts, directions and destinations clearly marked. Having disciplined himself to bring his material, which may previously have been a buzzing confusion of good but barely related ideas, under control he can now set to work polishing, rearranging, adding and subtracting, striving to improve the form and content. The process may reveal gaps in the preacher's knowledge which will have to be made good in order to ensure continuity and logic. A certain amount of looking up, rereading and searching may be necessary to supply the missing links in the chain.

The outline, besides providing a framework which will make the actual delivery easier, will ensure that the sermon contains clear argument and is free from woolliness, meaningless statements and those *non sequiturs* which throw the hearers off course.

Introductions and conclusions

Introductions

Let us suppose that the preacher now knows what it is he wants to say. He has organized his material and structured it so that it hangs together in a coherent fashion and makes some kind of logical sense. He may now find that to launch immediately into his first point would make too abrupt a beginning and be likely to take his hearers by surprise. What he needs is an introduction. In shaping his introduction he will be guided by several considerations.

In the first place, he will realize that his opening sentences will inevitably convey something about the preacher himself. Ideally they will immediately give his hearers confidence in the preacher. They will gather that he is well prepared mentally and spiritually for this moment. They will perceive that he has a word of God for this congregation and that he knows what he is about from the point of view of sheer technique. Only careful preparation will enable him to make a firm and decisive start. Nothing is more calculated to prejudice the effectiveness of a sermon, however good in other respects, than a fumbling, uncertain, apologetic beginning.

In the second place, the first few sentences ought to convey something about the topic of the sermon. If the hearers immediately perceive that the time is going to be spent in considering some matter of supreme importance which deeply concerns them then the level of attention will be such as to carry them at least as far as the first main point. If, however, they gain the impression that it is something rather trivial, of no more than superficial concern, then the level of interest aroused will be correspondingly low. For example, the hypothetical sermon mentioned earlier might begin simply with the great credal statement, 'I believe in the forgiveness of sins', followed by an invitation to reconsider what a tremendous affirmation it is to make. This could be followed by a sentence or two to show that this is not just one article of our faith amongst others. In a sense it is the whole of our faith. Within the space of a few seconds the hearers will be primed for what is to follow.

Thirdly, the introduction will convey some hint or even a plain statement (but not an outline, see below) of how the preacher proposes to treat his subject. This information or intimation will again create the conditions which determine whether or not the full attention of the hearers is carried right into the body of the sermon.

Fourthly and perhaps most importantly, the introduction can and should create in the hearers both an eagerness and a readiness to receive what the preacher is going to say. This last point, which really includes all the others, needs further explanation if it is to guide the work of the preacher in selecting appropriate material for his introduction.

It has to be remembered that each hearer has a mental world of his own. That mental world is composed of ideas, concepts, assumptions, attitudes, information, theories, problems, interests and so on. Only some of these are present to his consciousness at any one time but they will inevitably form the background and the framework for whatever new ideas are presented to him. It could be said that a sermon has its effect by interacting with whatever happens to be uppermost in the minds of the hearers at the time. From this interaction new meanings and new insights can emerge. The preacher aims to do just this and he will want to know how he can enhance the process.

The function of the introduction is to mobilize whatever concepts, ideas and feelings are already established in the hearers' minds but which are not just then uppermost. The introduction should call up those key ideas which will have the best chance of interacting with the sermon material to produce the effect the preacher wants. The pattern of ideas and feeling which predominates in the minds of the hearers at the time is a crucial factor in how new ideas are received. So the introductory material will be selected on the basis of its suitability to perform this function. The preacher will try to say something which creates that state of mind which will ensure that the sermon material is incorporated into the thinking of his hearers.

Many devices are available which can perform this mobilizing, motivating and organizing function. The preacher will need to experiment here with different introductions for the same sermon. It is often, but not always, a good idea to start with a biblical text. Alternatively a topic or area of human experience or a doctrine will be given out. This may be followed or preceded by a statement of a real problem, some curious fact, an interesting encounter, a topical event, an aspect of personality, a wise saying, an offbeat statement, a news story and so on. Whatever it is it should be brief, simple and pointed if it is effectively to mark out the ground, and create the right conditions of reception. Introductions which are long drawn out are often boring, uneconomical of time and usually ineffective. While it is sometimes possible to state the main headings of the outline in abbreviated fashion the preacher should never attempt to outline his outline. The outline of the structure of the sermon is for the preacher's own consumption not that of his hearers. They do not want to hear the sermon twice over.

Conclusions

Sermons, unlike old soldiers, should not just fade away. They should come to a definite finish. The finish should be 'built in' and not just 'allowed to happen'. All that has been said in the discussion about structure suggests that a sermon will have a distinct and definite aim of realizable proportions. It will be directed toward some perceived goal. This may be the creation of a new insight or the extension of an existing one. The intention may be to bring the hearers to the point where they are called upon to make a specific decision or resolve. It may be that the aim was to modify some attitude in the direction of Christian ideals. It is the function of the conclusion to pinpoint this target.

When he has made his points it is time for the preacher to bring into sharp focus all that he has been trying to say. The sermon in the end should provide the opportunity for the hearers to make a response.

The conclusion should mark the point where the preacher, as it were, stands aside and leaves his hearers face to face with the truth. He should aim to leave them in a confrontation which requires them to make a movement of the inner spirit toward that truth, if they will, or to know what it is they are rejecting if they fail to respond. The kind of response implied will not necessarily be a big, once and for all decision for Christ. It may take the form of a quiet resolve to be different, to feel differently, to think differently in future. It may simply be a happy acceptance and acknowledgment of the illumination of experience or an elevation of spiritual perspective. Whatever it is it will have the nature of an affirmation of the Gospel and a renewal or extension of commitment to Christ.

The last few sentences of the preacher will do everything possible to capture that moment of decision in a memorable form, so that the hearers may retain it beyond the instant, so that it can become a part of them, firmly welded into their lives. Since the conclusion will determine the final effect a sermon has the preacher should give careful thought to its preparation down to the last detail.

The content of the conclusion will, of course, depend on the kind of sermon it is. A brief review, summary or recapitulation will serve to provide a mental map. Sometimes a single striking incident, quotation, or question may be all that is necessary to point the way to the response required. It should be brief and not appear to be another sermon or the opportunity may well be lost. If an illustration is introduced here it should be absolutely 'right' for the occasion. If it does not form an organic unity with the rest of the sermon the result will be only confusion and uncertainty. Resentment may even be aroused as the hearer finds it out of keeping with what has gone before. It should gather up the essence of what has been said and be 'of a piece' psychologically and spiritually with the rest of the sermon.

Illustrations

A separate section on illustrations placed after the discussion of structure may appear to imply that these matters are to be considered by the preacher in that order. There is, indeed, a fairly common assumption that the substance and structure of the sermon is completed first and only after that is it time to think of how to 'sugar the pill' or press into the plain bun of the sermon a few fat currants, i.e. illustrations. But, to proceed on the rule, 'First get the structure built and then go on to add the decorations', involves a major misunderstanding. The process of presenting the Gospel vividly and compellingly is not necessarily like that at all. The error lies in thinking of illustrations as 'additives' which give the plain prose of discourse that 'something extra'. In fact, plastering a dull discourse indiscriminately with imported illustrations will not make that discourse live as a sermon. While it would be wrong to say that illustrations should never be introduced afterwards simply to brighten up a discourse, it is being increasingly recognized that this conception of the process of sermon illustration is attended by a number of errors mainly because of its artificiality.

In order to arrive at a better understanding of the process it is necessary to widen the discussion to include all imagery. Illustrations as rather formal 'set pieces' are only one part of imagery. Imagery includes picture language of all kinds. Besides the easily recognizable 'illustration' which consists in the telling of a story, relating an incident, describing an experience, imagery includes also the single graphic word or phrase, metaphor, simile, analogy and allegory.

Attention has already been drawn to the error of thinking that images are used to decorate and attract while plain prose is used to elucidate and state the truth. It is equally mistaken to suppose that the use of images has only to do with the emotions while, by contrast, plain words and abstract statements present reality and appeal to the intellect. In fact, it is rather the case that plain words can only hint at reality. On the other hand images and symbols are capable of presenting reality—of expressing it directly to the consciousness of people in such a way that they can respond spontaneously to it. People do not normally think analytically. The currents of thought, feeling and imagination are not easily controlled by mere information and general propositions. People tend to think most readily in terms of specific things and particular situations, objects, events and people. Images move men more deeply than abstract statements. The preacher's art is not unlike that of the poet, which is to use words to evoke the images which move men.

Images then, which include illustrations as usually

understood, are not optional extras to be tacked on to the bare bones of intellectual propositions. They are, properly used, the very stuff of preaching. The whole of the Bible is full of powerful and evocative images. It is doubtful whether the Christian religion can ever be presented without imagery. What, for instance, could be used to present the Passion of our Lord other than the imagery (in these cases historical facts as well) of the broken bread, the thirty silver coins, the roar of the crowd, the scourge, the crown of thorns and so on? Similarly, what plain statement could move men like the picture of the father in the Parable of the Prodigal Son? The parables of the gospels do not function merely as illustrations of truths which can otherwise be expressed in plain words. Parables actually carry the truth into the hearts of the hearers. They cannot be separated from the truth they express. They present truth in an irreducible and unique way to the people involved in the living situation out of which they arose. As images they are capable, in their context, of bringing men to the threshold of insight and to the point of decision. This is why it is useless to try to explain parables. They are themselves their own explanation.

This is how it should be with the images, the illustrations used by the preacher. They should arise out of and be organically part of the truth on which he is for the present reflecting. To preach is not to teach a lesson or to give moral exhortation. It is to make a pronouncement, a declaration which has the power to widen and deepen men's minds, stirring their desire to know and understand, moving them to the discovery of the decision each must, in his heart, take. It follows then that a preacher's illustrations, be they extended stories, descriptions, quotations or simply a single winged word, should be an integral part of the logic of his discourse and not something tacked on, as it were, from the outside.

As a practical question it is right to ask, Where do such images come from and what can be done to create the store of 'raw materials' with which our deepest thought will interact to bring to birth images which will embody the insights vouchsafed and implant them in the minds of the hearers? There is no easy answer to this question. The preacher needs to work and pray for the 'seeing eye', the quick mind and the receptive ear. If his illustrations are to be adequate to express the fullness of the Gospel he must be constantly aware of and sensitive to the 'high matters of life'. He must become a keen observer of human experience in all its variety. Detached observation is not what is called for but intelligent and sympathetic participation in the concerns of individuals and society.

In his reading, which should be as varied as possible,[2] and in his listening, the preacher should be ready to receive anything that might stimulate and enrich his thinking about the Gospel. It is not desirable that he should always be on the lookout in a sort of mercenary way, for illustrations.[3] In thinking about the Gospel he should try to have in mind the particular people he knows, the particular experiences, facts, information, knowledge about events which happen to have come his way. Similarly in his dealings with people and in his reflections on circumstances he should try to have in mind the Gospel so that the two concerns interact and fuse in his mind, the one enhancing and illuminating the other. In time, with this set of mind, images and illustrations do not have to be sought for, or borrowed. They spring unbidden to the mind of the person who is prepared to be patient and to recognize the right image when it occurs.

To be able to choose the right images when they present themselves implies also a rigorous rejection of those which

[2] See chapter 9.
[3] See chapter 7, p. 125.

do not measure up to the standards and functions that have been described. Caution in the use of illustrations is to be more pressingly urged than liberality. There is no need for the preacher to make 'heavy weather' of this matter, but a number of warnings about the kind of error which can creep in to the preacher's attempts to find the right imagery should be kept in mind.

Consider, for example, an illustration which was introduced into a passage about how lives can be redirected through meeting with Christ. The illustration consisted in the notion of light rays being bent in new directions by meeting objects and liquids (refraction). The trouble with this as an illustration is that it does not arise out of a deep understanding of what is meant by redirected lives. It is merely a gloss on the dictionary meaning of the word 'redirected'. It has no spiritual penetration at all though superficially it appears to serve as an illustration.

The unconsidered use of illustrations is bad not only theologically but psychologically. It has been pointed out that people are more prone to be influenced by images than plain intellectual argument. Unless, therefore, an image has some kind of organic unity with the trend of thought being pursued by the preacher, what appears to be a good illustration may have the effect of starting a train of thought in the minds of the hearers which is quite different from that of the sermon. In this case the more vivid and evocative the image the more it is likely to divert attention away from the argument rather than towards it. The illustration may only serve to 'run away with' the attention of the hearers. It is always difficult to avoid this, but it is more likely to happen if the image is not completely fused with the stream of thought being presented. This in turn is unlikely to be the case if the illustration has been brought in as an afterthought. For instance, the preacher might decide to illustrate something from an experience in an air raid. If his hearers have also had experiences of air raids the powerful image may divert their attention for the next few minutes by causing them to become preoccupied with their own reminiscences. It is necessary for the preacher to be aware of such possible side effects.

Other unsought effects are also possible, for instance, when illustrative matter is of doubtful truth and accuracy or otherwise puts a strain on credibility. The hearers may be more interested in resolving or disputing the illustration than they are in the preacher's intention. Furthermore, the introduction of such doubtful material can leave the insidious suggestion that the truth it was intended to illustrate is equally open to serious question. Similarly illustrations which are just trivial carry with them the unspoken suggestion that the preacher's topic is equally unworthy of serious consideration.

It should be remembered that no illustration or image is absolute. The truth is always bigger than the image. If an illustration serves to illuminate one aspect of the truth it may equally well conceal other aspects. An unsought by-product of some illustrations will be to bind the mind of the hearer to one aspect of the truth and to lead him to mistake the part for the whole.

The preacher should be on his guard against the long drawn out illustration which bores everyone before the end is in sight and which is extremely uneconomical of time. Some preachers draw illustrations from what their friends, family and acquaintances have done or said. The illustration may be such as to make it possible to identify the person(s) concerned. This should be avoided at all costs. It is likely to cause embarrassment for all and is open to the serious objection that confidences appear to have been betrayed.

If illustrations are drawn from the preacher's own

personal experiences without involving others directly they should be absolutely authentic and not 'dressed up' for the occasion. The danger here is that the preacher's own integrity might be impugned. The too frequent use of such illustrations may also lay the preacher open to the taint of exhibitionism. Even the suspicion of such things attaching to a person will nullify his effectiveness as a preacher. He may as well save his breath.

These warnings about some of the pitfalls in sermon illustrating are not intended to deter the local preacher in training from attempting to present his message vividly. They are intended as tests whereby the wheat can be unerringly sifted from the chaff. The impression may have been given that the process is more difficult than is sometimes realized. This is a right impression but with patience to wait for the right image to emerge from deep attentiveness to what the Gospel is about and an acute awareness of how people think and what their greatest needs are, the preacher will find the communicating word.

Useful Books

The ABC of Preaching—D. N. Francis (Epworth 1968)
The Ministry of the Word—R. E. C. Browne (S.C.M. Press 1958)
Something to Declare—B. J. N. Galliers (Epworth/ S.P.C.K. 1969)
Preaching Today—D. W. Cleverley Ford (Epworth/ S.P.C.K. 1969)

11. Preaching Technique

Paul Morton-George

IN THE sphere of preaching, technique can be a suspect word. It suggests something artificial, when above all we look for integrity, or something forced when we desire most to be free. But these misgivings are unfounded. Technique in any activity simply means that there is a right and a wrong way of doing it. We have to cultivate good habits and cut out bad ones. This involves discipline. No Christian should need telling that discipline is the road, not to restriction but to freedom.

All this is true of preaching. How often we say after hearing an outstanding preacher, 'He makes it all seem so easy'. Yet we know that the price of that apparent ease is hours of preparation and a hard discipline in method, language, voice and deportment. In short, his technique is good. Its discipline has given him freedom. This chapter deals with those factors which enter into the preparation and delivery of any sermon and which, to no small degree, decide whether it will be effective in the best sense, or not.

Manuscript and Notes

I IN PREPARATION

There are undoubted advantages (though dangerous pit-falls) in the practice of writing out a sermon in full. It is difficult to be critical of one's own style unless one can read it and 'hear' it as it is actually intended to be spoken. The tendency to wander on ('waffle') instead of making a point and moving on; a phrase that is not clear; an argument that is weak or illogical—all such things are exposed when written out, and can be corrected.

Checking Length

Most sermons are too long. For better or worse radio and television have conditioned us to give attention to one person talking for only limited lengths of time. They have also shown how much can be said effectively even in as little as five minutes. It is much easier to prune a sermon when it is written down. It is surprising (and often humbling) to discover how much better a passage sounds when reduced by half! A manuscript read *at the pace we shall use in the pulpit* also gives an accurate guide to how long the sermon actually is, and we can add to it or delete from it accordingly.

Seeing Structure

The previous chapter dealt with sermon structure. This is something which can be seen to be present—or absent—when material is written down. With nothing in black and white to refer to, we can persuade ourselves that the sermon does hold together like a good building, when in fact this is not so.

Illustrations are always the better for being written out and carefully worded. A good story can lull us so easily into thinking it will do its work without much thought given to it beforehand. This is quite untrue. Many an excellent illustration has been spoiled by careless phrasing. Sometimes the point is made too early, or the whole incident drags on until the congregation is heartily sick of it. But write out an illustration and ruthlessly prune it and we shall be left with one of the most effective instruments a preacher has.

All these things show the value of writing out a sermon in full. Certainly every beginner should submit to this discipline. But it has its attendant dangers to which we need to be alert.

Sermon—Not Essay

Perhaps the greatest of all is that we should produce not a sermon but an essay. There is a subtle but vital difference. An essay is meant to be written and read; a sermon is intended to be spoken and heard. An essay progresses smoothly on its way, but a sermon has an attacking, sometimes staccato note. This can be lost in the process of writing it down. It is best, therefore, to have a clear idea of how we are going to *say* something before we actually write it down. Preparing to speak should come before committing anything to writing, not the other way round.

Structure—Real or Apparent?

We noticed earlier that writing a manuscript can expose the structure of a sermon, or show its absence. Now it must be said that neatly written headings and sub-headings can be deceptive. They may suggest a structure which is not really there. We have to make sure that an idea which the headings suggest has in fact actually been worked out. This is one of the most searching self-criticisms we have to make. Written material is best for this purpose, but we

have to beware that it does not give a false sense of achieve-
ment.

Apportioning Time

The other danger of a full manuscript is simply that the
process is time-consuming. Our abilities vary greatly in
this. Some are quite used to committing their thoughts to
paper; others rarely do it in the normal course of events.
It is important to weigh up the time available and to use it
wisely. If writing out what we intend to say leaves us too
little time thoroughly to think our theme through, this
may be a case for writing out only key passages and using
notes for the rest. *But beware of using this as an excuse for
taking the way that involves the least effort.*

Preparing Notes

We shall be looking in a moment at the important question of what we take into the pulpit with us, but without
pre-judging that issue, the making of notes from the full
manuscript is essential to good preparation. In fact, a
rough and ready test of a good sermon is whether it
breaks down into note form naturally and easily. Certainly
beware of the sermon which does not!

These notes should consist of the main headings which
together show the argument and structure of what we
intend to say. Under each of these we need key words or
phrases as a reminder of the material under each heading.
The quantity of notes needed varies with each individual.
But avoid making them so full that they form a miniature
manuscript. Quotations, however, are best written out in
full, even in notes. And do make sure they are accurate.
So often they are not. Use a concordance to check Bible
passages and a dictionary of quotations for others. The
latter can be found in any public library.

Finally we have to make sure that we can see the notes

clearly from the distance we shall be from them when standing in the pulpit. Peering at notes is off-putting to one's self and distracting to a congregation.

II IN DELIVERY

Should sermons be read? The fact is that people who can read anything very well indeed are few—and a sermon should be read very well, or not at all. Another fact is that those who can read a sermon without its being obvious that they *are* reading it, are fewer still. This point is vital, since a sermon is intended to be preached. Preaching is proclamation. There is an 'attack' about it which is not meant to be there in, for example, a poetry reading, or the telling of a story.

The evidence therefore weighs heavily in favour of preaching from notes. But whether we decide to go into the pulpit with manuscript or notes, or even both, do make sure that the material is firmly anchored and can be turned over smoothly. A loose-leaf notebook, or one with a spiral spine, is better for the purpose than loose sheets.

An old lady once spoke her mind on a preacher's use of manuscript or notes. 'How does he expect us to remember what he says,' she demanded, 'if he can't remember it himself?' This was not quite fair, especially to local preachers, whose minds are preoccupied daily with quite different topics. But it does emphasize the need to make our memory aids as unobtrusive as possible.

'He spoke without a note.' How often this is said in surprise and admiration. Without being cynical, we may guess that the preacher in question had given that sermon many times before. And why not?—if it was a good one. But for most of us some memory aids are necessary, and we should feel no reproach at needing them.

Language

Some people have a gift for clear speech. But it can also be acquired. It is often a difficult road, but we must follow it. For if we cannot speak clearly about the things of God, it is far better to remain silent.

Follow Good Examples

In this, as in so many respects, Jesus himself has given us an example. Read his parables with this purpose in mind. Notice the economy of words, the absence of obscure ones, the terse summing up. What volumes are spoken, for example, by five simple words, 'Go and do thou likewise'. Many of the well-loved psalms are good examples to follow. Outside the Bible itself, read the work of writers like Winston Churchill, J. B. Priestley and most top-rank journalists. We should not *imitate* any of these examples. But steady reading of them makes some at least of their clarity 'rub off' on us.

Keep Sentences Short

A short sentence is clearer than a long one. Involved sentences lose our hearers faster than anything. Avoid parentheses at all costs. Make two or three phrases of them instead. This is an instance where a written manuscipt in preparation is so useful.

Choice of Words

We should never use a word unless we fully understand its meaning, or even if its meaning is only partly 'inwardly digested'. In social circles we all dislike name-dropping. Word-dropping by preachers, suggesting a spurious knowledge of the latest thought, is equally deplorable.

It is impossible to preach without using technical terms. Our faith has as much right to them as any other field of knowledge. But we have to remember that they *are* technical terms, some of which have totally different meanings in other spheres. Conversion means one thing to the preacher, and something else to a builder, a stockbroker or a rugger player. The same is true of familiar words of our faith like 'grace', 'redemption' and 'saved'. Our general rule therefore should be either to explain or paraphrase such words.

Grammatical mistakes and wrong use of words creep in very easily. For example, the word 'only' should come immediately before the word it qualifies ('He arrived there only yesterday'); there are 'kinds of persons' or 'there's a kind of person'—not a mixture of both. A word that is increasingly misused is 'disinterested'. It means 'impartial' *not* 'lacking interest in'. Columns such as 'Increase your word power' in the *Readers' Digest* are well worth studying.

Avoid the Cliché

Finally, beware of the ever-lurking cliché—the phrase or generalization which has been said or written so often that it has long ago lost any cutting-edge it ever had.

Be sure of this, no time spent on making our speech clear—and it does take time—is ever wasted. A kindly critic of one preacher made a surely justified misquotation of Scripture when she sent him a postcard which read: 'Though I speak with the tongues of men and of angels and have not clarity . . .'!

Voice

As some have the gift of clear speech, so some are endowed with a voice which comes over loud and clear. But whatever our natural endowments are, we must make ourselves heard. This is resoundingly obvious, yet still needs to be said.

Acoustics of buildings vary greatly. It is well to know as much as we can in advance about a church we visit for the first time, if only by enquiry in the vestry beforehand. Some churches have aural blind-spots (to mix metaphors somewhat!), which can be avoided after making such enquiries. Above all, remember that it is useless simply to talk to a congregation. We must 'throw' our voices to reach the back of the building. We should feel the words 'hitting' the back of our teeth and the roof of the mouth. Our words will not be heard properly until they are 'thrown out' to the listening people.

Microphones

Microphones are found in an ever-increasing number of churches nowadays. Unless one has an exceptionally good voice, it is better to accept the use of them. But we need to know something about them. Are they 'directional'— which will mean that whenever we turn away from them, the volume of sound emerging from the loud-speaker will drop abruptly? Or can we move about to a reasonable degree and still be heard?

Microphones should never be grasped (as a pop singer holds his) nor knocked against, as they do not discriminate between the human voice (or cough) and other sounds. If a microphone is in use, we have to modify our volume of speech accordingly. A loud voice amplified can become almost unbearable.

A final point to remember. Do make sure a microphone is 'on'. Find out about this beforehand.

Common Voice Faults

Even very experienced speakers have some fault which needs correction, and beginners may develop more than one. One of the most common is *monotony*. To a congregation this is either irritating or encourages slumber. In any case our material, however good, fails to register. Fortunately, there are cures for this fault which are fairly easy to acquire.

One is to *vary one's pace*. Linger over some sentences; take others steadily and quicken up in some others. The change brought about in this way from a monotonous delivery is remarkable, and refreshing.

Another cure is to *vary the pitch* of one's voice. Listen to a football commentator describing the players as they come on to the field, or a mother telling her child a story. Then hear the same man when a goal is scored, or the same mother exasperatedly telling the same child not to do something. If a musician were to write down the notes of their voices, there would be nearly an octave difference between the first speech and the second. Without imitating either of these examples, we can vary the note on which we speak to great advantage.

We can also speak *softly and loudly* at different points in a sermon. We can use the pause—but don't make it too long! All these things not only avoid monotony, but add light and shade to the delivery.

Two other faults need a mention. One is to *slur over the initial consonants* of words. 'And the 'eatest of 'ese is 'ove' is slovenly. 'And the greatest of these is love' is correct and effective. But far and away the most common failing is— dropping one's voice at the end of a sentence. Sometimes the listener can fill in the gap for himself, but often a key word is lost. 'What we need most of all is——.' Well, what *do* we need? No one knows, because at the critical moment the preacher's voice disappeared into his shoes.

This fault *must* be overcome. It is distracting and often tantalizing to the congregation. Fortunately, it can be conquered, though this may entail a little more discipline than in the case of monotony. What is needed is a *rising inflec-*

tion at the end of many sentences, instead of a falling one.
The note of the last word or two must be higher than the
rest. We often do this when excited. 'Just look at that
lightning!' (high note).

Testing for Faults

How can we make tests in order to detect voice faults
and to find out how far we have corrected them? One way
is to get the advice of a candid friend, and to heed it!
Another is to use a tape-recorder. We must find a room
where we can *preach* part of a sermon undisturbed and
unembarrassed. We tape our speaking, and then play it
back. Once the initial shock of hearing ourselves as others
hear us has passed, we can learn a great deal.

Deportment

The role of a preacher has a very high status—not because
of any virtue of his, but because he has what both Jesus
himself and Paul called a 'treasure' to offer. He should
therefore be dignified. But he must never stand on his
dignity.

This will govern the first thing a congregation will
inevitably notice about a preacher—what he or she is
wearing. We cannot dictate personal taste, but we can say
that dress should be dignified and not distracting.

A note should be given about gowns. First, to clear up a
misunderstanding. All gowns do *not* indicate that the wearer
has an academic degree. Vergers wear gowns; so do some
chapel-keepers. Choirs are sometimes gowned in our own
churches. The Geneva gown, worn by many preachers, is
not an *academic* gown. A good case can be made for its use
by all preachers, whether lay or ministerial. Like men's
evening dress, it is uniform, making all look (more or less)
alike. It covers lounge suits and dresses. It is an outward

sign of an office not lightly bestowed by our Church. Nevertheless, in some areas there is still strong feeling against what is thought—quite wrongly—to be nothing more than imitating High Church practices. In such circumstances it would not be wise or charitable to insist on wearing a gown.

Deportment includes movement. Too much movement in a preacher is distracting. If we tend to 'charge about', restraint is called for. But no movement at all can give an impression of lifelessness. Indeed, that impression may be correct. If we can preach the Gospel with scarcely a movement, has it really come to life for us?

Much the same applies to gestures. Overdone, they do more harm than good. But, for example, can we really cry, 'He is risen!' and not raise an exultant hand? Blows and even taps on the pulpit, made for emphasis, should be used with care, if at all. Remember, too, that microphones and amplifiers are merciless with such sounds, making them grotesquely loud.

Every preacher has mannerisms. Some are innocuous, some are an essential expression of the preacher's personality. Others have considerable nuisance value. Consult that candid friend again. He will say whether our particular foibles help or hinder, or are neutral in their effect. Too many good sermons are spoiled by mesmerizing mannerisms. We must get rid of them.

Finally, we should look our congregations in the face. It is not easy, and can be disillusioning. Sad to say, some of our best listeners are fidgets or apparently deep in slumber. But for a preacher to show a close interest in the pulpit desk, or the far corner of the church roof, is very distracting to a congregation. They may even wonder if the preacher is fully aware of their presence. So let us take our courage in both hands and face them, or at least appear to face them. Preaching, after all, is an 'I—Thou' relationship. Deportment can destroy this from the outset—or establish it.

Useful Book

Preaching—James S. Stewart (Teach Yourself Book, English Universities Press 1955), chapter 4.